SAGGISTICA 2

The Hyphenate Writer

and

The Legacy of Exile

edited by

Paolo A. Giordano

The Hyphenate Writer

and

The Legacy of Exile

edited by

Paolo A. Giordano

BORDIGHERA PRESS

Library of Congress Control Number: 2009905033

Cover design: Deborah Starewich

© 2010 by the Authors

All rights reserved. Parts of this book may be reprinted only by written permission from the authors, and may not be reproduced for publication in book, magazine, or electronic media of any kind, except in quotations for purposes of literary reviews by critics.

Printed in the United States.

Published by
BORDIGHERA PRESS
John D. Calandra Italian American Institute
25 West 43rd Street, 17th Floor
New York, NY 10036

SAGGISTICA 2
ISBN 978-1-59954-007-8

CONTENTS

Paolo A. Giordano • Introduction (xi)

Anthony Julian Tamburri • The Italian/American Writer in "Exile": At Home, Abroad, Wherever! (1)

Peter Carravetta • Problems of Interpreting Across Cultural Boundaries (26)

Jeffrey S. Librett • Abstraction and Materiality in Post-Holocaust Art: Colette Brunschwig's Collage Series *White Pebble for Paul Celan* (37)

Debora Cordeiro Rosa • Diaspora and Identity in Latin American Jewish Writing (58)

William O. Deaver, Jr • Three Waves of Immigration: Waving (Wavene) the Flag of Patriotic Fervor (67)

Humberto López Cruz • Cuban; American Literature: Suspicion of a Rupture in the Assimilation Pattern? (85)

Gustavo Pérez Firmat • Growing Old Bilingual (98)

CONTRIBUTORS (109)

INDEX (112)

Introduction

Introduction

In his 1951 book, *The Uprooted*, while writing on the great migrations of the late nineteenth and early twentieth centuries that created America, Oscar Handling penned the following words: "I shall touch upon broken homes, interruptions of a familiar life, separation from known surroundings, the becoming a foreigner and ceasing to belong ... the history of immigration is a history of alienation and its consequences." Today, we are witnesses to waves of migrations that have reached epidemic proportions. Many countries around the world are experiencing large-scale social and demographic changes that will probably alter their social fiber forever. These large-scale changes make immigration one of the most important issues in today's world, a world made smaller and almost borderless, by the seamless and instant transfer of information across the world wide web. Our senses are flooded on a twenty-four hour basis with arguments for and against globalization, free trade, news of international banking conglomerates, and of industries whose interests span the globe. However, in this frenzied movement of capital, of buying and selling assets, of mergers, in the rush toward a borderless world, there seems to be one item left behind, the human being. At Walmart, Cosco, Target, and other such stores we can choose from a myriad of goods from China and Honduras, out season fruit from Chile and Israel, wine from South Africa and Australia, but the human beings are largely forgotten. The message is, "We love your cheap labor, but we don't love you. Your bodies, especially the darker ones, need to stay where they are and keep on greasing the wheels of the new and improved borderless world."[1] This is a twenty-first century view but emigration, exile, expatriation have been part of the human existence and consciousness from the beginning of recorded time.

With this in mind we at UCF organized the one-day colloquium, *The Hyphenate Writer and the Legacy of Exile*. This volume collects the essays presented at the colloquium on February, 2008. This colloquium was born from an

---

[1] John Brady and Robert Soza, "Introduction: Immigration and Diaspora," *Bad Subjects* 60 (2002): http://bad.eserver.org/issues/2002/60/editors.html.

ongoing discussion we have been having for over twenty years on the themes of exile and immigrant writing, hyphenation, cultural boundaries, the breaking of such boundaries, and bilingualism: An ongoing conversation that becomes more complex with the passing years. The colloquium was divided into three parts: Anthony Julian Tamburri and Peter Carravetta examined the topic from an Italian American perspective; Jeffrey Librett and Debra Cordeiro–Rosa wrote on the Jewish *diaspora*; William Deaver and Humberto Lopez wrote about Cuban writers in the United States; and Gustavo Perez Firmat closes the volume with his essay on living and growing old bilingually.

Anthony Julian Tamburri argues that Italian Americans interested in their culture–in who they are, where they came from–need to be more serious and progressive when engaging in discussions about their culture, which, for the majority of them, is an amalgam of early twentieth-century Southern Italian peasant culture and American culture. He states, quite forcefully, that Italian-American writers and producers of culture need to go beyond personal reminiscences that lead to a nostalgic recall of the past, they need to revisit the historical past, "ask the hard questions, figure out what is good and bad about the culture and reconcile it with the present." Peter Carravetta's essay, "Problems of Interpreting Across Cultural Boundaries," is the beginning of a larger, more complex work on hyphenated poetry, migrant texts, and translations, themes that he has been working on over the last two decades. In this essay Carravetta introduces us to a panoply of approaches to be discussed and developed when trying to interpret across cultures and interacting in varying degrees with all the elements that constitute culture.

In "Abstract and Materiality in post Holocaust Art," Jeffrey Librett examines Colette Brunschwig's attempt to "articulate her painterly thinking with (Paul) Celan's poetic project" through a number of collages, in a context that is both a response to Emmanuel Levinas's 1972 essay "Paul Celan/De l'ètre a l'autre," and the necessity to read these collages as "that of the tension between figuration and abstraction in modern art generally and post-Holocaust art specifically." Debora Cordeiro Rosa, a young promising scholar, tackles the problem of identity, memory and assimilation within the Jewish *diaspora* in the works of three Latin-American authors, the Argentinians Marcelo Birdomajr and Isidoro Blaisten, and the Mexican born Marco Glanz. The novels and short story in question have as a unifying theme the devastation of assimilation and the crisis of identity, i.e. what does it mean to be a Jew.

In "The Waves of Immigration," William Deaver considers the consequences and legacy of Cuban exiles since 1959, when the first wave arrived on the shores of Florida. Deaver argues that as time passes, and generations come and go, we see the gradual disappearance of Cuba and Cuban enclaves in America as the setting for their works, and a move toward more regional settings void of references to Cuba. Deaver then develops a comparison between Cuban history and exiles with the fate of the Southern States after the Civil war and draws similarities between the children and grandchildren of Cuban exiles and Southerners. Humberto Lopez's essay, with the provoking title "Cuban; American Literature" explores divergent visions of the Cuban-American dilemma in the writings of two individuals, Roberto G. Fernandez and Virgil Suarez, both born in Cuba but who came to the United States at a very young age. Lopez concludes his essay with a final and very interesting consideration on the role of the hyphen.

The collection ends with Gustavo Perez Firmat's eloquent essay, "Growing Old Bilingual," that explores the burden of bilingualism, and how the work of a bilingual, bicultural author is inflected by the passing of time, and how the passing of time changes our relationship with the "languages we speak or write." As we get older, our native language lips away from us. Firmat uses many sources to develop his argument but emphasizes the case of the Franco-Argentine novelist Héctor Bianciotti, who, at a certain point in his life, stopped writing in Spanish and began to write solely in French. But in the end, Firmat concludes that "once bilingual always bilingual."

Dulcis in Fundo—This event could not have been possible without the support and generous contributions of Prof. José Maunez Cuadra, Director of the Latin American, Caribbean and Latino Studies Program; Professor Bruce Janz, Director of the Center for Humanities and Digital Research; Professor José Fernández, Dean, College of Arts and Humanities; and The National Italian American Foundation (Washington, DC).

Paolo A. Giordano
UNIVERSITY OF CENTRAL FLORIDA

The Italian/American Writer in "Exile"
At Home, Abroad, Wherever![1]

> *There is no ontology without archeology!*
> –Felix Stefanile

As my title clearly signals, any sense of "exile," be it literal or metaphorical, that is perceived by or discussed about any cultural broker of Italian Americana (read: artist, critic, essayist) is tri-fold in origin. First, there is the issue of provenance, so to speak; namely, What is the country of origin's interest in the well-being of the Italian/American writer? Second, there is the question of endpoint; and in this regard I am referring to the idea of the host culture, which for us is mainstream USA; so that we are apt to ask, "What is the interest, if any, of the USA's dominant culture with regard to the hyphenated writer of Italian origin? Finally, there is the issue of the in-group–i.e., Italian America–and how it perceives and, ultimately, receives or rejects the concept of Italian Americana as a valid cultural terrain within a larger, collective USA cultural landscape. That is to say, "How do we look at ourselves?"

While I do not presume to offer any answers to any of the above inquiries, suffice it to say that we shall never move forward in creating the group "narrative" that Robert Viscusi so eloquently discussed in his ground-breaking essay, "Breaking the Silence: Strategic Imperatives for Italian American Culture."[2] There, he spoke to the articulation of history, one that is not so much complete, as it is brought forward and discussed in all of its many facets: one that includes

---

[1] With regard to the slash (/) in place of the hyphen (-), see my *To Hyphenate or Not to Hyphenate: The Italian/American Writer: Or, An Other American* (Montréal: Guernica, 1991). A second point to underscore is the use of the truncated form, "Italo-", which, in its own right, deserves more space than can be dedicated here. For more, see *To Hyphenate or Not to Hyphenate*, 46.

This essay is a conglomeration of ideas that have appeared in different fora in both English and Italian: "Gli americani italiani e l'alterità: Meditazioni e propositi" in *Italian/American Cultural Politics* (Naples: Edizioni Scientifiche Italiane, forthcoming), and "Second Thoughts On The Diasporic Culture Of Italians In America: Here, There, Wherever." *Italica* 83.3-4 (Fall-Winter 2006): 720-28.

[2] See his essay in *Voices in Italian Americana* 1.1 (Spring 1990): 1-13.

a collective purpose, if ever so general, of Italian America. To date, this simply still does not exist. While much progress has been made on such issues, many Italian/American associations, as well as individuals, still work within a vacuum, so to speak, moving forward alone on issues that, in the end, would benefit the community at large and–especially as a group of regional and national organizations–would most likely have greater success in moving forward a variety of projects that would contribute to an Italian/American agenda.

The general question at hand may also be articulated in another manner. What is–or, what should be–that rallying point around which the greater Italian/American community might find some sense of commonality? We might say that African Americans, Jewish Americans, and Irish Americans have that one issue, as tragic as it may be respectively, that to some degree or another coheres the group. I have in mind, of course, slavery and its dreadful sister of outright discrimination that has resulted from it, for the first group; two millennia of *diasporic* existence and the recent, horrific holocaust, for the second group; and, for the third, the tragic, six-year potato famine of 1845 that sent over a million Irish to the United States during that time.[3]

What then can we identify as that cohesive force for Italian Americans? Can we look to something like immigration as the Italian/American rallying point? By immigration, I have in mind that historical period of 1880 to 1924, those forty-four years that have now become a sort of historical marker for Italian Americans of the twentieth and twenty-first centuries. There may indeed be more specific incidents, indeed tragedies, that come to mind–one being the 1891 New Orleans lynching, for which Italian Americans hold the dubious distinction of having been victims of the largest single lynching.[4] A second historical marker involves the enemy alien classification of the 1940s. After the December 7, 1941 attack on Pearl Harbor, President Franklin Delano Roosevelt implemented what was became known as the "Alien Enemy Act." Accordingly, non-United States citizens, though permanent residents of the

---

[3] There are clearly many positive aspects about each of these cultures that clearly contribute to each group's coherence. However, we surely do not err in seeing these more tragic events as the more cohesive element.

[4] This, of course, should not diminish the fact that of all the lynchings on record that have taken place in nineteenth- and twentieth-century United States, seventy percent were perpetrated against African Americans.

United States, were to be interrogated, their backgrounds investigated, and, if deemed necessary, interned. While such a *lawful* [in-]justice of the enemy alien status for Italians was rescinded on a fateful (and are we say paradoxical) October 12, 1942, it has taken decades, indeed a lifetime, for some members of the Italian/American community to speak out about this experience. In fact, we might be surprised to know that a majority of our community is rather ignorant of this historical tragedy.[5] For a third possible cohesive force that might rally Italian Americans, one might even attempt to underscore an historical discrimination, valid to be sure, dating back to the nineteenth century and culminating, to date, in something like the cable show *The Sopranos*.[6]

These last three examples are indeed worthy points of discussion and criticism. However, they do not constitute, in an overall encompassing manner, that one issue that can–and I would add should–unite the Italian/American community in the same way in which the three above-mentioned groups cohere. We might, in this regard, ponder what is that one all-encompassing issue that unites, for example, Hispanic Americans. To be sure, in addition to a strong sense of belonging that Hispanics may have with regard to their culture(s), it may very well be the migratory experience of the Hispanic–in spite of the various reasons for each geopolitical group's discreet emigration from the homeland–that sense of not belonging in the new host country, that coheres the group. Having said this, I do not want to be naïve in thinking that Hispanics from any and all Latin countries have an equal sense of allegiance to the old as well as the new country. Nor do I want to imply that all Hispanics have an automatic sense of belonging to that group comprised of Hispanics/Latinos, as we call them in the United States. Nevertheless, I do believe we

---

[5] For a chronology of governmental documentation, see the following website: http://italian.about.com/gi/ dynamic/offsite.htm?site=http://www.foitimes.com/internment/chrono.html. For more on the history of this unspoken event, see Kay Saunders and Roger Daniels, editors, Alien Justice: Wartime Internment in Australia and North America (St. Lucia, Qld.: University of Queensland Press, 2000); Lawrence DiStasi, editor, *Una Storia Segreta: The Secret History of Italian American Evacuation and Internment During World War II* (Berkeley, CA: Heyday Books, 2001) and Steven R. Fox, *UnCivil Liberties: Italian Americans Under Siege during World War II* (Boca Raton: Universal Publishers, 2000 [1990]).

[6] For more on this see, Salvatore LaGumina, *WOP: A Documentary History of Anti-Italian Discrimination* (Toronto: Guernica, 1999; originally published 1973). Let us, in the meantime, keep in mind that discrimination for discrimination's sake should not be an end product. Victimization unto itself is, in the end, counterproductive.

would not err entirely in believing that there is indeed a sense of commonality to some degree, and that this sense of commonality has its origins, to some extent, in the migratory experience in so far as they perceive themselves to some degree, in this country, as *outsiders*, and, for the most part, have decided to hold on to their culture of origin; first and foremost, this is manifested by their continued use of Spanish as their primary channel of communication, whereas Italian Americans have all but lost their use of Italian as a communicative agent.[7] This combination of difference and cultural specificity–based in part on the migratory experience–figures as a cohering agent to be sure.[8]

A similar formula might also prove valid for the Italian/American community–that emigration/immigration, in the broadest sense of the term, could surely figure as that cohesive agent that binds the group as a whole, however tenuous.[9] That is, a strong sense of commonality is indeed that necessary ingredient, I would submit, for the community to progress, for the study of all things Italian/American to become part and parcel of the dominant culture (or at least recognized as a valid *extra*-genre of United States cultural productions, if you will), as it is with the other hyphenated groups within the United States. All of this, of course, is dependent on the members of the Italian/American community to engage more fully in the appreciation of their culture. This entails an active participation in cultural activities of all sorts; it requires that Italian/American groups make a concerted effort to go beyond those one or two activities they have identified as their own, and make attempts to expand their agenda for it to include a new, more encompassing form of cultural integration. All of this, as we shall see, is dependent on a combination of cultural awareness and appreciation: namely a new sense of the Italian/American self

---

[7] Some may want to see the enemy alien act of 1942 as a major contribution to the loss of Italian in subsequent generations. On December 11, 1942 permanent residents who were not naturalized US citizens had to register with the United States government if they were still citizens of Germany, Italy, or Japan, the three countries considered at that time enemy nations to the United States.

[8] In stating all of this, I am patently aware of the many differences among Hispanics who come from difference geo-political areas. However, I believe we would also be naïve if we did not also realize the cohesive affectation of things Hispanic.

[9] Indeed, the above-mentioned tragedy of the Italian as enemy alien needs to be an integral part of this historico-sociological category of Italian emigration/immigration. We simply need to educate both the Italian/American community as well as both the United States community at large in North America and the Italian community in Italy. Ignorance is simply unacceptable that this historical juncture.

that leads, in the end, to an appropriation of one's cultural legacy and its overall impact on today's contemporary life, which ultimately calls into question the individual's ability to negotiate said legacy within his/her own Italian/American quotidian existence.

It remains indeed difficult, I would submit, to ascertain the level of interest and subsequent prospects of success within the United States–both within and beyond the geo-cultural borders of what we know of as Italian America–as well as in Italy, at least in these recent years, with regard to cultural productions of– in the spirit of avoiding a contentious term at the outset–Americans of Italian descent. I use this term at this time especially because there are still those in the United States who call them "Italo-americans" and, similarly, those in Italy who call them "italoamericani," both terms somewhat problematic and–if only with regard to its denomination–still debated in some camps. Elsewhere, I have opted for the term "Italian American" as noun and "Italian/American" as adjective, two terms that in Italian would be translated as "Americano Italiano" as noun–indeed debatable–and, something that many would surely consider a "mostriciattolo di appellativo" (a little monster of a name) "Italiano/Americano" for the adjectival form. There would be much discussion about an analogous term in Italian. Such a couplet, composed of two independent terms, might indeed be joined by a diacritical mark, if not joined together as one word, as is the case not only with "italo-americano," which becomes "italoamericano" but also with other terms such as "afroamericano" (o "afro-americano"), for instance. I would add at this point that the Italian term "americano italiano" is more than an accepted analogy to the English "Italian American" as noun.[10]

I have already discussed at length the *ragion d'essere* and, I would add, necessity–at least in English–of such a term and its coincidental issues regarding the hyphen.[11] We should not simply cast it aside with statements such as "quante discussioni, forse un po' oziose, intorno a quel fatidico trattino! Da qui

---

[10] Each term respects the grammatical logic (read, rules) of its respective language. For more on this notion, see my *Una semiotica dell'etnicità: nuove segnalature per la scrittura italiano/americana* (Firenze: Franco Cesati Editore, 2009) passim.

[11] In *To Hyphenate or Not to Hyphenate*, especially 20-27, 33-42, I also approach, among other things, the necessity of a more representative term for *Italophone* culture in the United States.

in poi, per semplicità, lo aboliremo" ("how many discussions, perhaps a bit tedious, about that fateful hyphen! From now on, for simplicity, we're going to abolish it."), as one Italian journalist turned literary critic/historian has declared.[12] Such a dismissive attitude is demonstrative, I would contend, of an intellectual diffidence–indeed, theoretical lethargy–that cannot add, in any constructive manner, to a still much needed critical-theoretical discourse on Americans of Italian descent and the various modes in which they are represented.[13] Further, such diffidence also suggests a lack of intellectual curiosity if not, to be sure, commitment to the field of *cultural studies*, which, I would submit, with specific regard to Italian Americans, readily transforms itself into a type of socio-political lethargy that, for a second time–especially after our forbearers were forced to leave their native country–lashes out against Americans of Italian descent. It is, in fact, precisely their socio-historical specificity of subaltern that is cancelled out, something we might suspect already occurred in the nineteenth century when, for many of the dominant culture, they were considered *colored*.[14] They become, so to speak, invisible for a second time, because the critical discourse remains simple and superficial. This said, then, it should become apparent that today we can no longer enjoy the privilege of ignoring such theoretical problematics that lie at the base of much discourse dedicated to both historically non-mainstream as well as dominant culture aesthetic forms of representation of Americans of Italian descent.[15]

---

[12] See Francesco Durante, *Italoamericana* (Milan: Mondadori, 2001) 5.

[13] Of course, here, for economy's sake, I intend both how they represent themselves and how they are represented by others both within the US and in Italy.

[14] Such cultural-historical erasure becomes increasingly evident as new studies appear. Furthermore, one might also say the same for Italians in the United States for the twentieth century. I have in mind Lawrence DiStasi's long-fought struggle to bring attention to the internment of Italians in the US during World War II. See his *Una storia segreta* (Berkeley: Heyday Books, 2001).

[15] I should state at the outset, especially since the tone of these reflections tend toward the critical, that I would be remiss not to mention those few who have proven to be steadfast in their interest, and therefore diffusion, of Italian/American studies in Italy. I have in mind the Fondazione Giovanni Agnelli, its pioneering journal *Altreitalie*, and its members, led by, especially, Madalena Tirabassi. For more on the Foundation and it's impact on the study of Italian Americans, see my "Italian/American Critical Discourse: Studies for the New Millennium with A Little Help from Our Friends!" *Altreitalie* 20.1 (2001): 23-42.
    Claudio Gorlier, in turn, has contributed to the recognition and, dare I add, validity of such a category if only because of his many reviews and essays on the subject matter. Others would include: Simone Cinotto (food), Simona Frasca (popular music), Paola Casella and Giuliana Muscio (cinema), Stefano Luconi and Adele Maiello (history). My intention is not to paint American Studies either in Italy or in the United States

FROM ITALY TO THE US: OR, WHAT DO THEY THINK OF US?

With regard to American Studies in Italy, we can grasp a fairly clear picture of how Italian/American Studies fares in the Italian academy. The Italian journal, *Ácoma*, for example, published in its first eighteen issues, spanning seven years (1994-2000), two essays dedicated to Italians in America, both of which are translations of essays that had already been published in the United States; the first an abbreviated version of a three-year-old essay, the second a complete translation of a two-year-old essay.[16] The mention of such editorial practices does not intend to impugn any sort of negligence to this or other journals of American Studies in Italy that emulate such low frequencies and importations. However, one might expect, indeed hope, that such attention paid to Americans of Italian descent is not limited to a recycling and translation of what had already appeared earlier in the United States.[17] Indeed, this was remedied, we might say, the following year; in issue 19, *Ácoma* published three essays dedicated to, respectively, Don DeLillo, Louise de Salvo, and Pietro di Donato and John Fante.[18] More recently, however, it seems the journal has taken a step, let us say, sideward in this regard; under the rubric *Schede*, in which Italian scholars speak briefly to the recent state of the art, the journal lists five ethnic literatures of the United States: "La letteratura degli afroamericani" (The Literature of Afroamericans), "La letteratura indianoamericans" (The Literature of Indianamericans), "La letteratura asiaticoamericana" (The Literature of Asiaticamericans), "La letteratura ebreoameri-

---

with one brush; rather, to look at those nooks and crannies that could readily be revisited, with the aim of examining further a greater consciousness overall among "americanisti" in both countries.

Finally, I would underscore that these thoughts, as the reader will realize, are limited to the literary, which explains any lack of reference to works in other fields, such as anthropology, history, sociology, etc.

[16] The essays are: Robert Orsi, "Il colore dell'altro: confini, religione, identità in mutamento tra gli italiani di Harlem", *Ácoma* 5 (1995): 5-12, and Rudy Vecoli, "Emigranti italiani e movimenti operai negli Stati Uniti. Una riflessione personale su etnicità e classe sociale", *Ácoma* 5 (1995): 13-22.

[17] The key notion is here the "limited to" that I would underscore. The translation of what has developed in the US is, I would submit, extremely significant for the further development of an intellectual discourse in Italy on Italian Americans. Much has already been done, especially if one takes into consideration those books published on the subject matter by SUNY press as well as Mary Jo Bona's study and Edvige Giunta's collection of essays. See further notes 18 and 22 of this study.

[18] See *Ácoma* 19 (Spring-Summer 2000): Alessandro Portelli, "I rifiuti, la storia e il peccato in *Under-world* di Don DeLillo" (4-15); Caterina Romeo, "*Vertigo* di Louise de Salvo: vertigine della memoria" (33-9); Martino Marazzi, "Pietro di Donato and John Fante" (55-9).

cana" (The Literature of Jewishamericans), "La letteratura dei *Latinos*" (The Literature of *Latinos*).[19] The lack of an Italian/American category only adds to the assumption that a significant part of American Studies in Italy may indeed still look upon the writings of Italian Americans with a somewhat disinterested eye. Such an assumption is bolstered, I would contend, by members of the journal's editorial board. In their introduction to the monographic section entitled, "L'America che leggiamo: saggi e aggiornamenti," in a 2006 issue of *Ácoma*, Sara Antonelli and Cinzia Scarpino write:

> Di particolare urgenza, e in linea con le scelte editoriali che caratterizzano "Ácoma", risultano poi i discorsi legati alle tante componenti ethniche e sociali del tessuto culturale statunitense ai quali il presente numero dedica una serie di interventi dal formato più agile. A essere messi in rilievo sono qui i diversi percorsi che, sulla scia dei vari "Rinascimenti" politici e letterari degli anni Settanta e Ottanta (*Latinos* e asiaticoamericani), hanno portato le diverse letterature d'America a elaborare le esperienze delle minoranze storicamente oppresse (Afroamericani, Nativi Ameri-cani). Un discorso a parte meritano, infine, gli Ebrei-americani, le cui opere vengo-no recepite di volta in volta come interne o esterne alla produzione *mainstream*.
>
> [Of particular urgency, and in line with the editorial decisions that characterize *Acoma*, there are thus those discourses, tied to the many ethnic and social components of the United States cultural fabric, to which the current issue dedicates a series of essays in a more agile format. Highlighted here are the various trajectories that, in the wake of the various political and literary "Renaissances" of the 1970s and 1980s (*Latinos* and Asiaticamericans), have brought forward their different literatures of America to elaborate on the experiences of the historically oppressed minorities (Afroamericans, Native Americans). Jewish-Americans, in the end, warrant a special discussion, their works having been perceived from time to time as either internal or external to mainstream production.][20]

---

[19] See *Ácoma* 31 (Spring-Summer 2006).
[20] See, Sara Antonelli and Cinzia Scarpino, "L'America che leggiamo," *Ácoma* 31 (Winter 2005): 19. A curious aside—indeed hopeful with regard to a broadening of horizons vis-à-vis *hyphenated* literature—may be found in Armando Gnisci's *Creolizzare l'Europa: Letteratura e migrazione*. (Rome: Meltemi, 2003). With regard to Italian migration literature, that which is written in Italian by the "new" immigrants to Italy, he wrote: "[N]oialtri italiani dobbiamo imparare a imparare dal nostro passato migratorio, oltre che dalla breve

First of all, one would be hard-pressed not to include Italian Americans among the "the many ethnic and social components of the United States cultural fabric "; for better or for worse, Italian Americans are constantly represented in the various media as US ethnics. Second, Italian/American writers could readily fit into at least two of the three categories above. Indeed, a "Renaissance" of Italian Americana, especially literature and film, has already manifested itself, if only by the increased critical activity both from within and outside the Italian/American community.[21] In turn, because of writers like David Baldacci, Don DeLillo, Lisa Scottoline, and Philip Caputo, to name a few best-sellers, Italian Americans might also deserve "a special discussion, their works having been perceived from time to time as either internal or external to mainstream production." Third, and a debatable point, indeed, there are some who would insist that Italian Americans went through their own period of oppression and discrimination; one need only recall the New Orleans lynching of 1891.[22] Finally, as we continue to read, the pages of this issue constitute an attempt to "tracciare una mappa dei pieni e dei vuoti di un territorio complesso che invita

---

ad esagerata (in tutti i sensi) esperienza di potenza coloniale, ad avere a che fare con il presente interculturale, in casa e dovunque nel mondo. Quest'ultima considerazione ci aiuta, infine, a formulare in maniera più compiuta la rivendicazione di una letteratura italiana della migrazione. Essa deve essere pensata innanzitutto come un fenomeno della modernità avanzata, senza precedenti. Inizia con le migrazioni di intere popolazioni di italiani verso tutto il mondo alla ricerca di lavoro a partire dall'immediato periodo post-unitario e trova il suo completamento nella letteratura scritta dagli immigrati, venuti in Italia da tutto il mondo in cerca di lavoro, a partire dall'ultimo decennio del XX secolo" (83; "We Italians have to learn to learn from our migratory past, beyond the brief to exaggerated (in every sense) experience of colonial power, to dealing with the intercultural present, at home and wherever in the world. This last consideration helps us in the end to formulate in a more complete manner the claim of an Italian literature of migration. It needs to be considered first and foremost as a phenomenon of advanced modernity, without precedent. It begins with the migrations of entire populations of Italians throughout the world in search of work, beginning with the immediate post-unification period, and it finds its completion in the literature written by immigrants, having arrived in Italy from all over the world in search of work, beginning with the last decade of the twentieth century."). I thank Evelyn Ferraro for the reference to Gnisci's thought on this matter.

[21] From outside the Italian/American community, I would recall the 1987 special issue of *Melus* dedicated to Italian/American literature and film. This becomes most poignant precisely because it is not an Italian/American voice; rather, one dedicated to the study of "multi-ethnic literatures of the United States."

[22] See also, Salvatore La Gumina's *Wop*; Mathew Jacobson, *Whiteness of a Different Color* (Cambridge: Harvard UP, 1998) passim; Joseph P. Cosco, *Imagining Italians: The Clash of Romance and Race in American Perceptions, 1880-1910* (Albany, NY: SUNY, 2003); and Jennifer Guglielmo and Sal Salerno, eds. *Are Italians White? How Race is Made in America* (New York: Routledge, 2003), also available in Italy published by Baldini e Castoldi.

a una riflessione attenta ("trace a map of highs and lows within a complex territory that invites keen reflection")," and "l'accento dei contributi critici ... cade sui meccanismi che impediscono una fruizione e una comprensione più completa delle *letterature* e delle *culture* nordamericane" (19-20; emphasis textual; "the emphasis of the critical contributions ... falls on the mechanisms that impede a fruition and a complete comprehension of North American literatures and cultures."). By excluding any reference to the existence of the American writer of Italian descent within that kaleidoscopic cultural landscape that we know as the United States, only sets further back the articulation of any semblance of an Italian/American discourse in Italy.

An analogous case seems to exist with the publications of the AISNA (Associazione Italiana di Studi Nord-Americani [Italian Association of North-American Studies]); the association's official journal, *RSA* (*Rivista di Studi Nord-Americani* [*Journal of North-American Studies*]), has yet to include an essay on Italian Americana, from what I've been able to discern.[23] Its annual conference and subsequent proceedings, conversely, have regularly included sessions and papers on the subject. In fact, its 1985 proceedings of its 1983 conference are dedicated entirely to the theme "Italy and Italians in America."[24] Likewise, its 2001 conference dedicated to the theme "America and the Mediterranean" includes numerous essays dedicated to Italian Americana.[25] Such a distinction in publishing fora speaks volumes, to be sure, in every sense of the word. It also underscores, I would contend, the presumed reasons why

---

[23] The journal, an annual, was first published in 1990. The actual issues are difficult to consult, given certain challenges presented by the national library system in Italy. Nevertheless, AISNA has listed on its website most of the tables of content and, for the earlier issues, essays in MSWord or PDF format, allowing for easy access to most of the journal's articles.

[24] "Italy and Italians in America," edited by Alfredo Rizzardi, *RSA Rivista di Studi Anglo-americani*. Anno III, N. 4-5 (1985), published by Piovan Editore, 1985. There is, as the reader will notice, a slight difference in title between the "journal" and the "proceedings"–*Rivista di Studi Nord-Americani* vs. *Rivista di Studi Anglo-americani*–thus constituting a bit of a challenge when seeking our either. In addition, while the "proceedings" carry the title of "rivista" from volume to volume, they carry instead an ISBN number and are produced by different publishers.

[25] *America and the Mediterranean*, edited by Massimo Bacigalupo and Pierangelo Castagneto (Torino: OTTO editore, 2003). It seems that from the 15th conference on, the proceedings now appear as discreet volumes. I would also note that the publisher OTTO editore has indeed a series *nova americana* that includes a number of volumes dedicated to Italian Americana.

writers such as David Balducci and Lisa Scottoline had originally published in Italian as, respectively, David B. Ford and Lisa Scott.

ITALIAN AMERICANS WITHIN A UNITED STATES CULTURAL LANDSCAPE

Literary and film criticism dedicated to numerous other *diasporic* groups in the United States has, to be sure, developed its own type of theoretical discourse, creating indeed a general mode of thought processes that, for the most part, form part of an overall intellectual articulation of the group under consideration.[26] What stands out when one attempts such an inventory is the conspicuous absence of Italian/American literature as one of the many categories that make up bibliographies, be they written or virtual. One website, associated with a university, lists nine categories, four are general while the remaining five are group-specific (General Background, African-Americans, Asian-Americans, Hispanic-Americans, Jewish-Americans, Native-Americans, General Background on Literature, Critical Theory, Literary Terminology). See, Research Guide to Ethnicity and Identity in Literature (http://www.wcsu.edu/library/gd_ ethnic_lit.html). Since such an omission occurs at the national level, we should then not be surprised that it repeats itself on an international level. See, American Literature on the Web: Minority Literature/Multi-Cultural Resources (http://www. nagasaki-gaigo.ac.jp/ ishikawa/amlit /general /minority.htm).

Such a methodological-theoretical discourse and coincidental inventory have yet to develop with regard to Americans of Italian descent, be it here in the United States or in Italy. Obviously, the primary benefit from inclusion in such inventories is visibility. In Italy, for example, desired visibility of this sort

---

[26] A list of primary examples would surely be close to exhaustive as well as most debatable. Nevertheless, I offer up a few names and titles dedicated to the study of other multicultural literatures: Bonnie Tusmith, *All My Relatives: Community in Contemporary Ethnic American Literatures* (Ann Arbor: U Michigan P, 1993); A. LaVonne Brown Ruoff, *American Indian Literatures: An Introduction, Bibliographic Review, and Selected Bibliography* (New York: MLA, 1990); Ronald Takaki, *A Different Mirror: A History of Multicultural America* (Boston: Little, Brown & Company, 1993); Ramon Saldivar, *Chicano Narrative: The Dialectics of Difference* (Madison: U Wisconsin P, 1990); Carl Shirley and Paula Shirley, *Understanding Chicano Literature* (Columbia: U South Carolina P, 1988); Houston A Baker, *Singers of Daybreak: Studies in Black American Literature* (Washington, DC: Howard UP, 1974); Henry Louis Gates, *The Signifying Monkey: A Theory of Afro-American Literary Criticism* (New York: Oxford UP, 1988); Juan Bruce-Novoa, *Chicano Poetry: A Response to Chaos* (Austin: U Texas P, 1982).

initially lies in such publications as those mentioned above.[27] In the United States, conversely, there are three journals dedicated to Italian Americana that regularly publish essays, creative works, and reviews.[28] And while they serve a major purpose—they are the primary organs for the dissemination of works by and about Italian Americans—they are not, nor should they be, the *ne plus ultra*, the ultimate solution vis-à-vis the larger, cultural landscape of the United States. Not until essays on the subject matter appear in journals such as the *American Quarterly, American Review*, and *American Studies* can those dedicated to Italian Americana rest more easily; otherwise, we remain in our own little ghetto.

Indeed, some *infiltration* into mainstream United States culture has already been successful; for the past fifteen years a handful of university presses and American studies journals have published or republished significant work.[29] In this sense, then, a good part of a foundation has been laid. But much more has yet to be done. In perusing the last eight annual addresses of the American Studies Association, for example, it is a curious fact that, among all the topics mentioned dealing with issues immediate also to Italian Americana, there is no mention at all of Italian/American studies, not even an occasional, oblique reference to the ethnic origin of an American writer of Italian descent.[30] Such an absence of attention raises a number of issues, and to some

---

[27] I would again remind the reader of *Altreitalie*, for a long time the only venue where one could readily find writings in both Italian and English dedicated to the various cultures of the Italian diasporas, especially in the rest of Europe, the Americas, and Australia. See the journal's website at: http://www.altreitalie.it.

[28] They are: *Italian Americana, The Italian American Review*, and *Voices in Italian Americana*.

[29] Some examples include: SUNY Press series in Italian/American Studies, directed by Fred Gardaphè; Josephine Gattuso Hendin's "The New World of Italian American Studies," *American Literary History* 13.1 (2001): 141-57, or Thomas Ferraro's less conspicuously titled essay, "'My Way' in 'Our America': Art, Ethnicity, Profession," *American Literary History* 12.4 (2000): 499-522; other mainstream press books include: Mary Jo Bona. *Claiming a Tradition: Italian American Women Writers* (Carbondale: Southern Illinois UP, 1999); Edvige Giunta's *Writing with An Accent: Contemporary Italian American Women Authors* (New York: Palgrave, 2002); as well as Gardaphè's earlier pioneering *Italian Signs, American Streets. The Evolution of Italian American Narrative* (Durham: Duke UP, 1996). Most recently, Thomas Ferraro published *Feeling Italian* (New York: NYU Press, 2005), Robert Viscusi published *Buried Caesars* (New York: SUNY 2006), and Fred Gardaphè published his *From Wiseguys to Wise Men* (New York: Routledge, 2006). Let us not forget that the first study to be published in this area was Rose Basile Green's *The Italian-American Novel* (Madison, NJ: Fairleigh Dickinson UP, 1974).

[30] The addresses are: Janice A. Radway, "What's in a Name? Presidential Address to the American Studies Association," *American Quarterly* 51.1 (March 1999): 1-32; Mary Kelley, "Taking Stands: American Studies at Century's End: Presidential Address to the American Studies Association," *American Quarterly* 52.1 (March 2000): 1-22; Michael H. Frisch, "Prismatics, Multivalence, and Other Riffs on the Millennial

degree, adds yet another challenge. For while there are a number of excellent books in English on Italian Americana,[31] what is still missing, for example, is a rigorous study that, first, examines those whom we might consider the major writers of Italian Americana and, second, then contextualizes them within the greater, United States literary panorama in which we normally situate the corresponding great "American" writers.[32]

HOW DO WE SEE OURSELVES?

Within the Italian/American community, as it remains ever so relevant on a national level, race is one of a few issues we still need to explore–interrogate, if you will. This question of race, I would further contend, is twofold in nature and scope. It deals with, on the one hand, how Italians in America (read, Italian Americans) have been considered, portrayed, and treated throughout the long history here within the United States. One might readily argue that the twentieth-century plight of the Italian (read also, Italian American) began back in 1905, at the onset of the motion picture industry; one need only hark back to silent films such as F. A. Dobson's *The Skyscrapers of New York* (1905), Edwin Porter's *The Black Hand* (1906), and D. W. Griffith's *The Avenging*

Moment: Presidential Address to the American Studies Association," *American Quarterly* 53.2 (June 2001): 193-231; George Sanchez, "Working at the Crossroads: American Studies for the 21st Century - Presidential Address to the American Studies Association," *American Quarterly* 54.1 (March 2002): 1-23; Stephen H. Sumida, "Where in the World Is American Studies? Presidential Address to the American Studies Association," *American Quarterly* 55.3 (September 2003): 333-352; Amy Kaplan, "Violent Belongings and the Question of Empire Today: Presidential Address to the American Studies Association," *American Quarterly* 56.1 (March 2004): 1-18; Shelley Fisher Fishkin, "Crossroads of Cultures: The Transnational Turn in American Studies: Presidential Address to the American Studies Association," *American Quarterly* 57.1 (March 2005): 17-57; Karen Halttunen, "Groundwork: American Studies in Place" *American Quarterly* 58.1 (March 2006): 1-15; Emory Elliott, "Diversity in the United States and Abroad: What Does It Mean When American Studies Is Transnational?" *American Quarterly* 59.1 (March 2007): 1-22; Vicki Ruiz, "Citizen Restaurant: American Imaginaries, American Communities," *American Quarterly* 60.1 (March 2008): 1-21.

[31] For a review of what was available until and through the first half of 2003, see my "Beyond 'Pizza' And 'Nonna'! Or, What's Bad about Italian/ American Criticism? Further Directions for Italian/American Cultural Studies," *MELUS*. 28.3 (2003): 149-74. To this list, one would add at this juncture Robert Viscusi's *Buried Caesars* (2006), and Fred Gardaphè's *From Wiseguys to Wise Men* (2006).

[32] Other questions are begged at this point. What should be, if at all, the relationship between Italian Studies and Italian/American Studies in the United States? Should intellectual outlets–journals and book series– dedicated to Italian Studies open their doors, so to speak, to Italian/ American essays and creative works? To date, if memory does not fail me, two Italian journals in United States have already done so: *Forum Italicum*, *Italian Culture*, and *Italica*.

Conscious (1914), each of which may figure as early, *good* candidates as the springboard for such stereotyping; the Italian character in this third film–played by a non-Italian, as was often the case–is an ill-reputed blackmailer.[33] Themes such as sex, violence, sentimentality, family relations, and the like will seem to dominate the cinema of and about Italian Americans, generating a most contested debate, within the Italian/American community at the end of the 20th century about the portrayal of Italians and Italian Americans in United States media in general. In fact, even in his earlier film, *At The Altar* (1909), Griffith seemed to raise concern within the dominant culture by underscoring, in an apparently positive story-line, sexuality and violence as part of the Italian character. To be sure, both aggressive behavior and sexuality ultimately figured as two components of the Italian and Italian/American character as cinema developed, within the first half of the 20th century, in the United States. Be it the gangster films of the 1930s, which laid the foundation for the violent mobster, or the oversexed individuals of the later years, the Italian male will, in many respects, ultimately culminate in a figure such as Tony Soprano, a violent, oversexed capo-regime whose sexual proclivities bring him to the edge of seducing his own nephew's fiancé, Adriana.

On the other hand, we need to call into question the issue of how race is perceived, processed, and treated by a certain component of the Italian/American community. We need only to think back to the two infamous episodes of the 1980s, Howard Beach and Bensonhurst. These were two tragic sites of racial strife that involved to varying degrees the Italian/American community. Yet, so it seems, the majority of the then leaders of the Italian/American community remained silent on the issues. Yet, again, the counter-demonstrations did nothing but underscore the fairly widely perceived stereotype of the Italian American as racist, bigoted, and, ultimately, capable of engaging in dumbshow, as a number of Italian Americans countered the protests of the African-American community with vulgar gestures, racial epithets, and the despicable display of watermelons, as the African-American contingency marched down the streets of Bensonhurst. Two people spoke up in print. Immediately after

---

[33] For earlier negative depictions, see LaGumina's *Wop*, cited above in note 6.

the Brooklyn tragedy, Jerome Krase, then professor of sociology at Brooklyn College, wrote an op-ed in *Newsday*. A few months later, Robert Viscusi, also of Brooklyn College, published his above-mentioned essay in *Voices in Italian Americana*, in which he laid out a series of "strategic imperatives" for Italian/American culture.

One of the primary steps that members of the Italian/American community need to take is to re-visit our history. It is a record that is rich with achievements and successes. It is also a record that lists a series of sad and tragic events and episodes that have befallen our own turn-of-the-twentieth century Italian Americans. But, it is also a record that, as the more recent cases of racial strife have demonstrated, has also proven at times to be inimical to the racial challenges that blacks have had to confront throughout the years. Such challenges, so it seems, have often been seen as "their" problems. But, as the history of Italian America proves, they have also been "our" problems. During the first half of the 20th century, actually since the onslaught of the major wave of immigration (1880-1924), Italians, like other southern Europeans, were perceived as non-white in this country. Indeed, as stated at the outset of this essay, while it is true that blacks constituted the largest group of people lynched, Italian immigrants have that dubious distinction of being the largest group hung at one time. The alliance between Italy, Germany, and Japan during WWII placed many immigrants on an enemy aliens list. One unspoken negative consequence, for sure, was the loss of what would seem to have been the subsequent generation's linguistic inheritance. "Don't speak the enemy's language" clamored the innumerable posters and other public announcements during that time. Furthermore, Italians were underutilized in numerous professions over the years, and in more recent times when it now seems we have become *white* and, consequently, respected members of the upper middle class, things have not improved as one might have wished.

These are some of the reasons we need to revisit our history. Let us not forget that, according to what we might surmise from the behavior of some in the entertainment world, Italians are sometimes still fair game for ridicule in the public arena. We cannot always take for granted that we enjoy all the benefits of those who inhabit on a daily basis that world of WASP-dom. This, I would submit, is still not the case in spite of the wonderful successes of those past and present, including our current Speaker of the House, who broke both ethnic and gender boundaries, "at a single bound," as the old TV show proclaimed about Superman. Joey of *Friends*, George of *Seinfeld*, and the Romanos of *Everybody Loves Raymond* are three examples of what some might consider more recent negative portrayals of Italian Americans in the medium of television.[34]

WHERE MIGHT WE GO FROM HERE?

In his by now classic essay, *Race Matters* (1993), Cornel West suggested that the "fundamental crisis in black America [was] twofold: too much poverty and too much self-love" (63). I wonder if we might not be able to say that the *problem*, if this is the right term we might want to use, within Italian America is "too much [affluence] and [not enough] self-love," to borrow from West.

Strong words, some might say. Problem? What problem, since many Italian Americans run major companies–national and international–and some of our best writers, for example, are of Italian descent? This, indeed, is, I would contend, part of the problem. The affluence among Italian Americans has led them out of the city and into the suburbs, thus believing that all is well, all obstacles have been surpassed, and we can now move forward. With such an

---

[34] Remedy to some of the above was sought out and obtained by individuals in the past. The late New York state senator John D. Calandra and colleagues took it upon themselves to investigate the treatment of Italian Americans–faculty, staff, and students–at the City University of New York in the 1970s, since there had been numerous complaints about the treatment of Italian Americans within CUNY. The finding was that Italian Americans were indeed under-utilized and under-represented at all levels university-wide. The immediate result was then Chancellor Kibbee's proclamation (December 9, 1976) that Italian Americans were to be considered a protective class throughout CUNY, with all the rights and privileges of the federally recognized affirmative action groups. Another result was the eventual formation of the Italian-American Institute to Foster Higher Education, in 1979, which, over the years, has been transformed, in both size and mission, into The John D. Calandra Italian American Institute, a university-wide, research institute under the aegis of Queens College, CUNY. The 1979 Institute was founded primarily to foster higher education among Italian Americans (through academic and career counseling especially) and impart, to both Italian Americans and non-Italian Americans alike, knowledge of the culture of Italian America. Over the years, the mission broadened, to include social, psychological, and demographic research on Italian Americans both within and beyond the walls of CUNY. Today, these earlier research components are now buttressed by an equally rigorous sector of cultural activities that range from lectures to symposia to film series. Such an institute dedicated to Italian Americana–be it the original structure of 1979 or the more expanded unit of today–is a unique entity. No other center or institute both here in the Americas or in Italy (the exception being the Fondazione Giovanni Agnelli of Turin) approaches its magnitude and the possibilities therein.

exodus, the various Italian/American neighborhoods (proverbial Little Italies and the like) underwent dramatic change. First of all, the younger members left, often selling off parents' homes and businesses to new immigrants, non Italian Americans, for which the various old stomping grounds, especially the Little Italies, turned into what many have recently labeled "Italian-American theme parks." Second, the original cultural artifacts and practices were willy-nilly transformed into commercial ventures, losing their original cultural and historical valence. A more recent example is the brouhaha over the San Gennaro festival of Manhattan's Little Italy, when a subcommittee of Community Board 2 rejected the application for the 79th annual San Gennaro Feast, reason being that no representative of the Feast appeared before the subcommittee. If "The San Gennaro feast is a very important tradition for the Italian-American community, and I hope to see it continue," as Ms. Derr stated when offering to postpone the vote so the application can be defended, one wonders why no one from the San Gennaro committee showed up in the first place to present the application. In addition, one surely wonders about the current cultural and historical valence of the feast; as the *New York Times* article, in closing, quoted an unidentified customer in a barbershop, "When I was a kid, the feast was about family, religion, and food. Now it's about CDs and three pairs of socks for $10" (April 15, 2007).

AFFLUENCE: There is no doubt that our *paesanos* have "made it" in all walks of life. Some of the more notable companies, national and international, have had and continue to have Italian Americans in positions of power. There are those who run major home-hardware companies, those who run major investment firms, those who run major publishing houses, those who run major medical companies, and those who are at the helm in significant governmental positions (in this case perhaps more *influence* than *affluence*), from local to national. Affluence, therefore, and, dare I say its inseparable twin, influence, are up front and present in the Italian/American community.

"And so what's your point?, one might readily ask. To be sure, there has been an admirable display of a certain type of philanthropy within the Italian/American community: various sectors of hospitals, endowed chairs in business and the sciences, and sports arenas have all been the beneficiaries of Italian/

American philanthropy. Where we are dramatically lacking, I would contend, is with regard to what I have labeled in conversations with friends, *book culture*. Here, of course, I use the term "book" as a wide-reaching label that necessarily includes the arts and humanities: classical and contemporary, high-brow and popular; figurative, performative, visual, and written. One example: Only in 2007 was there the announcement of a set of three buildings acquired for an Italian/American museum in New York City; and only in Spring 2008 did the building finally become property of the Italian American Museum. To date, a brick and mortar museum, *come Dio comanda*, as we might say in Italian, does not exist, though this most recent transferal of property keeps hope alive. The 1999 co-sponsored New York exhibition of "Five Centuries of Struggle and Achievement" (co-sponsored by the John D. Calandra Italian American Institute and the New York Historical Society, and primarily curated by the late Philip Cannistraro) was a wonderful project that ran for four months. It consisted of at least a half dozen rooms in which artifacts were displayed and, in some cases, living and travel conditions were reassembled in order for the twenty-first century individual to gain some sort of concrete idea of the conditions at the turn of the twentieth century. In all, it was an excellent exhibition, with an impressive catalog; it surely could have been the impetus from which to move forward in an expeditious manner. Instead, it has taken, so it seems, close to nine years just to get possession of property for a future museum. Basically, in all, we have had to wait more than one hundred twenty years for an independently standing Italian/American museum, whereas other United States ethnic groups got the job done well before we did.

AMOR PROPRIO: self-love, we would call it in English. One of the first steps, to be sure, which demonstrates that we possess a healthy dose of Italian/American self-love, is for us to be aware of our culture and its history. A second step is that, when the situation warrants, we are willing to bring forth the cause of Italian America, even if it means that someone from outside our community may indeed question our *modus operandi*.

One of the most egregious examples of one's unawareness is Gay Talese's 1993 essay, "Where Are the Italian American Novelists?" Until the appearance of this essay, Talese, to my knowledge, had never truly negotiated in any profound manner the cultural and/or intellectual terrain of Italian America, except of course for his 1970 bestseller, *Honor Thy Father*, a journalistic investigation into the history of the reputed Joe Bonanno, crime family. The book eventually earned Talese a great deal of respect in the world of print journalism and, around the same time, solidified his name as one of the founders of what was then dubbed "new journalism."[35] The type of activity that Talese exhibited in his 1993 essay on the Italian/American novel, nevertheless, resembles to some degree what I have previously dubbed as *intellectual ethnic slumming*: that is, a visitation upon the greater realm of, in our case, Italian America by someone whose quotidian space is, to the contrary, the *non Italian/American* world, and yet, every once in a while, decides to visit the *Italian/American masses*, so to speak, for an array of reasons, many of which are not always clear.[36] In his essay, Talese demonstrated precisely how misinformed he was at that time of the extent to which the Italian/American novel had already been in existence. The pioneering scholar Rose Basile Green had already documented the history of Italian/American novels in her 1974 study, *The Italian-American Novel*, both in the ninety-plus number of books she discussed within her main text and the more than two hundred entries of novels she listed in her bibliography.[37] The question then, for Talese, should have been not so much "where are the novelists?" but "why are the novelists ignored?" Talese himself, however, was obviously not familiar with the Italian/American fictional landscape, for which the more relevant and therefore exceedingly more significant question to pose did not form part of his semiotic horizon.

There is, more significantly, another side to the metaphorical coin of *ethnic slumming*, and it is Gramscian in content, to be sure. Namely, what are the *duties* and/or *responsibilities*, if any, of someone involved, however so slightly, in Italian Americana? Must this person take on that Gramscian role, or some

---

[35] The irony in Talese having written a book on the Bonanno family, however, is that today he seems to be one of the more vocal people against those who adopt similar themes (organized crime) in their work. All this appears to be a 1990s awakening on his part, which apparently coincided with the publication of his genealogical account, *Unto The Sons*.

[36] See my above-cited "Beyond 'Pizza' and 'Nonna'."

[37] See, Rose Basile Green, *The Italian-American Novel: A Documentation of the Interaction between Two Cultures* (Madison, NJ: Fairleigh Dickinson UP, 1974).

semblance thereof, of the "organic intellectual," or can (should?) s/he just go about his/her business and *do his/her thing* as the individual s/he is? This is, I would submit, one of the most important issues that impact our community, one that clearly deserves much greater attention from all of us.[38] It is, I would contend at this point, that second step required by one's sense of *amor proprio*. We need, for sure, to ponder further the issue of the group versus the individual, that person similar to a Gay Talese who has the ability (read, *cultural currency*) to further the group's cause. This is an age-old question that Italian Americans need to tackle since we can now readily say that we have, literally and metaphorically, arrived.

BI-CULTURAL ITALIAN AMERICA

Another significant characteristic of the Italian/American community is its bicultural and, to some extent, bilingual aspect. Indeed, within this *diaglossic* landscape there are those who, to use the verb in a transitive mode, "live Italy." Expressed in such a manner, the phrase *literally* refers to those who live within the geopolitical confines of the country, whereas *metaphorically* it may refer also to those who live the experience that is Italy and all that it pertains, but they do so beyond its geopolitical borders: namely, they embody in their manner of existence that geo-cultural sign we all know as Italy. Some members of this second group–those who "live Italy" but reside in the United States– seem to define themselves as Italians living abroad, even though their period abroad has been, to say the least, rather extensive.[39] Others, still, identify them-

---

[38] Various questions come to mind in this regard, some of which are: What are/should be the expectations of Italian/American orgainziations vis-à-vis the prominent members of their respective Italian/American communities? Do they, for example, perennially appear as "guests" of socio-cultural events such as fund-raising, formal events when just about everyone else must pay a significant "donation"? Should they be included in cultural events and projects when, at other times, such projects and events do not comprise part of their public biographies? Should they be given a sort of *carte blanche* when it comes to strategies concerning issues in which they are not professionally prepared? When do, we might also ask, they join group as individual, pulling their weight as everyone else?

[39] This reminds us of the self-described group of "Italian Poets in America," first presented as a category with the special issue of *Gradiva* 10-11 (1992-93). A good deal of literature has been written on this phenomenon of the bilingual Italian writer in the United States. It raises a series of issues, to be sure, that deals further, among other things, with labels, as the title of the special number of *Gradiva* suggests: "Italian writer in America," "writer in exile," "expatriate" are just some of the labels that circulate. In my own *A Semiotic of Ethnicity*, I saw this type of writer included in what I consider a later group of those writers who, though

selves a tad bit less generically as Italians in America. Sociologically speaking, however, since they have, for a significant period of time, inhabited a geo-cultural territory that is indeed the United States of America, the desire to opt for the appellative of "Italian" as opposed to the binomial "Italian American," might readily, to paraphrase a popular disco tune of the 1980s, make us want to go Hmmm. More seriously, it begs a number of questions, one of which might be: Is there something to the notion that for those who "live Italy"–while residing in the United States–there exists an inscrutable, sociologically semiotic mechanism of the Italian immigrant that springs into action, one who is identified with a certain period of United States history (1880-1924), for example, and who belongs, most likely, to a certain social class–proletariat, for lack of a more adequate term–with peasant origins and possibly illiterate?[40]

Strong words, indeed, some might say. But they constitute the thoughts and whispers of many, spoken "between us," on the QT, but never brought out into the open. It is the proverbial white elephant, the naked emperor, that which no one wants overtly to recognize. Yet, intellectually speaking, the label "Italian American" simply refers to a sociological category that refers to any person who leaves one country for another, with the intentions of remaining in

---

linguistically different, belong nevertheless under the greater umbrella of Italian/American writer. See chapter 7, "Italian/American Writer or Italian Poet Abroad? Luigi Fontanella's Poetic Voyage," of my *A Semiotic of Ethnicity: In (Re)cognition of the Italian/American Writer* (Albany: SUNY P, 1998): 109-17.

Other essays have been written on this phenomenon. One of the more acute contributions to the discussion is a recent essay by Andrea Ciccarelli, "Fuoricasa: scrittori italiani in Nord America," *Esperienze letterarie* 29.1 (2004): 83-104, where, in closing, he also raises the issue of Italian writing outside of Italy and its relationship to Italian literature. Previous significant essays and collections include, first and foremost, Paolo Valesio's "The Writer Between Two Worlds: The Italian Writer in the United States," *Differentia* 3 & 4 (Spring/Autumn 1989): 259-276; the relevant essays in Jean-Jacques Marchand's edited volume, *La letteratura dell'emigrazione: gli scrittori di lingua italiana nel mondo* (Turin: Edizioni della Fondazione Giovanni Agnelli, 1991); Peter Carravetta's insightful introduction to *Poesaggio. Poeti italiani d'America*, eds. Peter Carravetta and Paolo Valesio (Treviso: Pagus, 1993); and Luigi Fontanella's *La parola transfuga* (Florence: Cadmo, 2003).

[40] The "Italian" writers mentioned above have all, to some degree or another, dealt with the issue of their bilingual and bicultural sociological status in the United States. Two elder statesmen who have also championed their bicultural status are Giose Rimanelli and Joseph Tusiani, each of whom has composed prose or poetry in at least three languages (Italian, English, and dialect), with Tusiani also writing in Latin. Others, instead, seem not to have done so in any fashion, except, perhaps, in re-writing or translating their creative work into English. In any event, the many names that come to mind, both those who have and have not negotiated their bilingualism and biculturalism, might include: Luigi Ballerini, Emanuel Carnevali, Alessandro Carrera, Giovanni Cecchetti, Ned Condini, Rita Dinale, Franco Ferrucci, Arturo Giovannitti, Ernesto Livorni, Irene Marchegiani, Mario Moroni, Eugenia Paulicelli, Mario Pietralunga, Annalisa Saccà.

that second location. It is the basic coupling of two terms, a registry's description, so to speak, of the individual, in that the first term signals the country of origin whereas the second indicates the long-term country of residence. This said, then, the binomial "Italian American" should, as we all know, merely signal that Mr. or Ms. "So-and-so" is (1) either of Italian origin or was born in Italy and, if the latter, (2) now has been a resident for a significant amount of time in the United States.[41] The fact that there may be a semiotic that, at first glance, seems difficult to perceive–namely, that such a term has a peculiar connotation with respect to relocating from one country to another, *migration*, as mentioned above–clearly amplifies further the above-mentioned discussion on class and individual self-identification and ultimately complicates the issue for many involved.[42]

WHERE MIGHT WE GO FROM HERE?

Allow me to suggest possible remedies, modest to be sure, in the form of a series of questions that follow. First, why is there no section in certain bookstores, especially those larger establishments in a city like New York, dedicated to Italian/American writing? Why would a manager, owner, and/or corporate CEO shun such an idea? Given the thousands of square feet a bookstore occupies, what impact could a regular bookshelf (five to seven yards of space) of Italian/American books have? Second, why is it that of the six or seven of the dozen or so forthcoming books on the home page of a book publisher, the one title that is dedicated to Italian Americana does not appear? Does the director not think the Italian/American title warrants mention on the first page of the press's website instead of being relegated to the second page among the second half of the titles mentioned? Third, how is it possible that a book dedicated to United States poetry, one that seems to present itself as historically

---

[41] By significant amount of time, I have in mind no less than ten years during which time the individual is engaged in his/her daily activities, personal and professional, in his/her host country, even if there are frequent trips back to the country of origin.

[42] Might the possible referent here be the stereotyped imagine of immigrant of the early 20th-century, that short, dark-skinned, moustached individual who travels with the proverbial card-board suitcase with string around it?

analytical and prescriptive, does not include a chapter on any Italian American, not even someone like John Ciardi?

In an interview with author George De Stefano, I posed the question of responsibilities of those of us in positions of *authority* in our respective fields. His first words were, poignantly so, "cultural transmission."[43] We need to be sure that those who follow, the younger generation, are aware of our culture, past and present. They can indeed have access to such knowledge in two ways: (1) People need to be there to impart the information necessary for such cultural awareness. This includes teachers and professors, on all levels. Such a strategy for success is twofold: (a) people need to get into the various K-12 curricula lessons on significant Italian Americans. To date, the New Jersey Italian and Italian American Heritage Commission has a wonderful plan they are trying to get passed on a state level; (b) Professors at the college/university level need to include Italian Americana in their various courses and, especially at the graduate level, in their seminars. (2) This, in fact, leads to the second of two ways–an area where "push comes to shove," so to speak. This is where cultural philanthropy comes into play; professorships in Italian Americana need to be established; centers for Italian/American Studies need to be established. Both, clearly, can be done through endowments of approximately $2,000,000 and $1,000,000 respectively. Endowed professorships and centers run the gamut for other United States ethnic groups, funded by individuals and/or their foundations. Very few individuals among the Italian/American community have engaged in such cultural philanthropy; we can practically count the number on one hand.

What I have outlined above constitutes some of the reasons, I would contend, why the cultural world of Italian America might benefit from a more rigorous theoretical and methodological tune-up, one that takes into consideration both the creative and critical realms. Furthermore, and indeed for reasons slightly different, I would include both those in the United States as well as in Italy who study Italian/American cultural productions. Indeed, one of the major tasks of all who study cultural Italian Americana is to examine further

---

[43] See *Italics, The Italian-American TV Magazine Show*, episode 188.

the numerous factors that lie at the base of such culture, to seek out all possible answers to the various questions we might want, once again, to examine:

> Why, we might first ask, did so many of our forbearers have to leave Italy during those forty-plus years of the great wave of immigration? Because the south was miserably poor is indeed true. But is this, in itself, a satisfactory response?
> On the threshold of the third millennium, we find ourselves among fourth- if not fifth-generation Italian Americans. This said, may we not ask what sort of debt, if any, might contemporary Italy have with regard to those who have lived either directly–immigrants–or indirectly–subsequent generations–the migratory experience and its legacy among the later generations?
> What has Italy done over the past one hundred years to better the conditions that lead to the great exodus that began at the end of the nineteenth century?[44]
> What are, today, the roots of those aesthetic works–written and visual–that contribute to the cultural world of Italian America? Why are there, and not rarely, certain unpleasant images in many written and visual works, and yet the writer/ director feels the need to insert them into the work?[45]
> In general terms, then, what type of world do Italian/American artists represent in their works?

These are some of the questions for which we still need to seek out answers, even if such answers (1) are not easy to ascertain at first glance, (2) are not the clutch answers we might readily desire, and (3), further still, are not all positive and consequently do not contribute to a more sentimental overall picture of the immigrant experience. In an attempt to seek them out yet a second time, I would contend, we must pass over that critical threshold based primarily on biographical and accepted historical factors, as well as that which one assumes is based on the author's intentions. Or, as Joseph Sciorra characterized it, those "'common sense' histories and assumptions," which constitute an "uncritical and linear account of self-resolve, family cohesion, and religious conviction

---

[44] We might indeed ask what would have happened if the United States had imposed an earlier limit to Italian immigration?

[45] Two works I have in mind are Gianna Patriarca's *Italian Women and Other Tragedies* (Toronto: Guernica, 1994) and the more recent Italian film, *Come l'America*, dir., Andrea and Antonio Frazzi (2001). In both works one finds the angry immigrant who ends up physically abusing wife and children.

ending in the boardrooms and suburbia of white America[, which] involves a significant amount of memory loss and obfuscation of the historical record."[46] Finally, in order to complete the cycle, so to speak, we must also acknowledge that specific, historical patrimony of suffering, marginalization, and exclusion that many immigrants had to endure on both sides of the ocean, both in their country of origin, which eventually lead them to leave, as well as their country of arrival, which, as the apocryphal story goes, made them then pave the mythical "streets of gold."

We need, in the end, to learn to take our culture more seriously. We cannot continue to engage in a series of reminiscences that lead primarily to nostalgic recall. Instead, we need to revisit our past, reclaim its pros and cons, and reconcile it with our present. Namely, we need to figure out where we came from, ask those unpopular questions of both ourselves and the dominant culture, and continue to champion our Italian/American cultural brokers of all sorts—artists and intellectuals—so that they can continue to engage in an Italian/American state of mind, if such is their choice.

Ultimately, all of this is dependent upon our recapturing our own sense of *amor proprio* and combining it with our abilities—financial, performative, aesthetic, intellectual, etc.—in order to document, maintain, transmit, and further propagate our Italian/American culture; anything short of such activity is tantamount to failure.

Anthony Julian Tamburri
JOHN D. CALANDRA ITALIAN AMERICAN INSTITUTE

---

[46] See his review of *Heaven Touches Brooklyn in July* (2001) by Tony De Nonno. *Journal of American Folklore* 117.466 (2004): 459. He continues: "During the past twenty-five years, scholars and artists have begun to critique and dismantle 'common-sense' histories and assumptions by exploring topics such as the larger global Italian *diasporic* experience, Italian American involvement in labor struggles and radical left politics in the late nineteenth and early twentieth centuries, their support of fascism during the 1920s and1930s, especially among ethnic elites, patriarchal violence and intergenerational conflict, and the privileges of whiteness in a racist society" (459). Indeed, some of these hot points have already been addressed in, among others, the following essays and books: Stanislao Pugliese, "The Culture of Nostalgia: Fascism in the Memory of Italian-Ameircans," *The Italian American Review* 5.2 (1996/1997): 15-26; Philip V. Cannistraro, *Blackshirts in Little Italy: Italian Americans and Fascism, 1921-1929* (Lafayette: Bordighera Press, 1999); Jennifer Guglielmo and Salvatore Salerno's *Are Italians White?*.

Problems of Interpreting Across Cultural Boundaries

Let me begin with an anecdote. In 1973, having graduated from City College in New York, I set out to study for a year at the University of Bologna. It was a momentous decision, made all the more intriguing by the fact, which I should introduce for the anecdote to make sense, that I was born in the province of Cosenza and arrived in the US in 1963. For all intents and purposes, though, in 1973 I considered myself an American from the Bronx who spoke a strange dialect at home, but did those things that proletarians and working class youths typically do, from holding all sorts of part-time jobs to planning various career possibilities when finishing college. I recall that often, whether in jest or during more tense encounters, someone would tell me: go back to where you came from, which irritated me to no end, since I took the newly learned myth of a country founded by pilgrims and immigrants and bent on liberty and self-affirmation to be the ultimate grounding truth of my society, and one which validated my identification with America. I managed to get through those highly volatile years in a society torn by student, labor and political unrest, focusing on a career in the sciences. Having in mind the cutting edge research conducted by NASA, one doable path meant enrolling in the US Air Force at the Manhattan College ROTC. But then one day, walking proud in my uniform, a student threw a rolled up piece of paper at me in disgust, accusing me of representing the nether side of America, siding with the angels of death that visited thousands in North Viet-Nam. After the initial dumbfoundedness, I did begin a process of re-evaluating exactly where I was going to position myself in life. I transferred to CCNY and there the Army ROTC was already burned to the ground and student protests took on a new meaning. Midway through college, I changed my major to literature. Upon graduating, I went to study in Italy, at the famous University of Bologna.

The Italy I was to experience was radically different from the distant Italy of my humble birth. I was in a vibrant, very politicized and bourgeois city with a different dialect, rich historical traditions and a highly literate culture. I remember the first week in September looking for an apartment, and being turned down repeatedly. For some reason, I would identify myself as a student from Calabria, figuring I would have an advantage over fellow students from both the US and many other Mediterranean countries. Then one day, well into my second week there, as I was showing a landlady my papers, she saw my passport: "Ma lei è Americano?" she said. Well, yes, I responded. Then no problem, I have a beautiful room you can share with someone else, for $ 40 a month.

Capital had won, ethnicity had lost. But national identity became suspect from that point on, and the politics of self and social representation entered the arenas of my mind for the next twenty years. The show continued, for in Bologna every other week there was a major rally by this or that political party. I was often accused by my new fellow students of being an "imperialist pig" simply because I came from America and so was associated with the Vietnam War, the oil embargo and support for Israel, and was called a "racist," because it was well known that in America they hated and mistreated the blacks. Oh, the ironies of history. The fact that I was also amidst the last emigrants out of the underdeveloped South to seek work and an education in a foreign country did not interest anyone, though people have repeatedly asked me ever since whether I consider myself an Italian, or an American, and most recently an Italian American, and in what language I think, or even dream?[1] The fact that I had worked through high school and college was not a story they wanted to hear. On the one hand, I started studying the canonical masters of Italian letters and culture, on the other, I was experiencing first hand, and in my supposedly native country, the stigma of otherness, difference, distrust, xenophobia and rejection, which in some ways was "logical" or "predictable" in the first new country I had arrived in, but literally blew my mind upon this "return."

❖

Interpreting across cultures does not refer exclusively to interpreting very far off and exotic texts and artifacts or, even more importantly, the sense of the ac-

---

[1] "Knowing the identity of one's country cannot be reduced to a mere matter of residence as 'insiderliness'," writes R. Radhakristnan in his *Diasporic Meditations, Between Home and Location* (Minneapolis: University of Minnesota Press, 1996) xxvi. Someone once asked Chinua Achebe in which language he had an orgasm!

tions of other peoples. For it can also refer to the problem of interpreting between and across texts and people from cultures not too different from our very own, and yes, even within our own. For if we only stop and think that America itself is an "invention," outside of a set of imposed institutions, laws and grammars, there might very well be little in common between third generations families from, say, San Diego, Hartford, CT, and New Orleans. And much the same can be said about people who for generations have lived mainly in locales like Udine, Livorno or Matera. Looked against the magnitude of the relative diachronic axis, I would say if being an American is a complex fate, being an Italian is closer to a nightmare.

Interpreting across cultures means literally *crossing*, and therefore *interacting with*, in varying degrees, class boundaries, epistemological axioms, ontological fields, normative grammars, stylistic preferences, language games, mythographic sequences, and conscious and unconscious ideologies–in short, dangerous territories and perilous seas, all of which compel the critic (the reader, the traveler) to make adjustments to his/her cognitive and expressive *apparati*, and attempt to understand his/her role in the post-post epoch we entered in 2001.

❖

This paper is a first sketch of a general introduction to a collection of writings on hyphenated poetry, migrant texts, and translation I plan on publishing as a book, to follow an earlier collection titled *Prefaces to the Diaphora*.[2] I begin by delving into the interconnections between anthropology, literature (in a very broad sense, to include all genres) and hermeneutics as they emerge when texts and other cultural artifacts highlight the very issue of *how* we talk *about* them, how we *attribute* meaning, how they "fit" somehow with our pre-conceptual understanding or whatever we unfailingly bring to the interpretive process. Above all, how both writer and critic represent the encounter of two worlds, and how meanings are generated in the exchange.

Specifically, it will look at, and juxtapose in a chiastic fashion, some recent contributions in ethnography and post-colonial studies, revise some hermeneutic tenets debated with in Continental Philosophy circles, compare/contrast how

---

[2] Peter Carravetta, *Prefaces to the Diaphora. Rhetorics, Allegory, and the Interpretation of Postmodernity* (West Lafayette: Purdue University Press, 1991).

each field has broken epistemological ground in order to better comprehend the other, and highlight the common problems, the topics upon which they converge, co-exist (not necessarily in harmony) and spin and stitch figures for a postmodern critique. One central argument is the understanding of the *rhetorical act*, which I argue must readmit to theorizing about language its *existential component* in order to assay how discursive forces jostle for efficacious positioning in a concrete dynamic spectrum that extends from immanent localism to transcendent globalism, cutting across disciplines and time frames. The dynamics of the rhetorical will shed light on a conception of language which saves, discloses, or permits the unspoken, the untranslatable, or the "residual" to be yet available for fruition and interpretation ... even in the age of the endless, frenetic criss-crossing of virtual messages, the age of Hermes.

Should the reader be listening for my underlying ontology or politics, let me state at the outset that I am aiming at rehabilitating the academic or the intellectual at large as a key player in the future of our society, one who must of course cherish no *a priori* ever suspicious universally "true" statements about the human condition, yet still believe in the possibility that there are given circumscribed areas in the social continuum wherein s/he can effect a constructive difference. I will argue between the lines for a para-sitic engagement at the locus of the borders or the interstices themselves, "involving the dense web of relations between coercion, negotiation, complicity, refusal, dissembling, mimicry, compromise, affiliation and revolt."[3] And I will speak against the notion of opposition and resistance in modernist and even some postmodernist versions insofar as these strategies, predicated upon a dualistic logic of opposites and contradiction, only reverse the order of the pre-emptying, strong logocentrism of the Western ethos, of power, imperialism and, to be precise, of colonization. I will argue, as I did in my 1991 book, that a primary component of the critical enterprise is to take chances, to risk, to step into the *agora* (even the virtual one) in order to effect a crossing which, if nothing else, compels the interlocutors to think, to re-consider, to re-enter the temporality of historical consciousness.

This requires that we reach outside the tepid precincts of our specializations, and intervene in public and political arenas: if war is too important to be left solely

---

[3] Anne McClintock, *Imperial Leather* (New York: Routledge, 1995) 15.

to the generals, education is definitely too important to be left nowadays in the hands of misinformed and possibly poorly educated politicians and career administrators. The ongoing discussion on whether we ought to teach creationism next to evolutionism should serve as a reminder that knowledge is ever and always politically marked and prone to misuse and abuse. In teaching at the freshmen level we inevitably find ourselves linking up with the "outside" world, and we find ourselves teaching stuff we can hardly claim to know as experts. The difference between what constitutes Knowledge and what goes under the label of Critical Thinking will constitute another background preoccupation to these remarks.

This outside world is extremely unpredictable and heterogeneous. The main concern here is how to interpret across cultures that are no longer distant in terms of either time or space, but whose actors, agents and representatives travel, mingle, contaminate and transform one another constantly, and how this may bear on education and politics. "Over determined as it is by multiple histories, the postcolonial location feels like an intersection, fraught with multiple adjacencies" (Radhakrishnan, xxvii).

Thus we hone in on hyphenated authors, border crossers, marginals, hybrid subjectivities and silenced socio-historical actors: women, prisoners, children, and all sorts of "aliens," from immigrants to expatriates, from refugees to silently disempowered individuals and groups. For another major problem is that of how to translate, how to re-create the discourse of these ... others (as opposed to the Other of our Western metaphysics). Here the suggestion is made that it is in the nature of the active, living–i.e.: rhetorical–utterance *both* to speak *about* something (which we can reformulate within an epistemologically fluid hermeneutics, such as we glean in ethnography and new Historicist criticism), *and* to conceal something else which cannot be even put into language but which nevertheless plays a role in shaping and nuancing active discourse (which includes here speech, song, writing, dialectic).

To explore fruitfully this second possibility–that of the residue, or noise, or *je ne sais quoi* of communication, and which deconstruction has unsuccessfully attempted to articulate, going as far as pointing out in given that there was a differance, but unable to do anything with it–we should assume that, as I argued in *Prefaces to the Diaphora*, perhaps language *tout court* is an allegorical process, one which embodies the epistemological *and* the ontological, the private *and* the public. Language is not simply or only a system of tropes more or less identifiable and describable (*speaking-of-others*, which is fine and contributes to the specific history of my themes and creation myths, and so on, relying on a time tested hypothesis about the allegory-symbol relation),[4] but also and more pointedly as an *other(s)-speaking* whose symbolic and semiotic network is either precluded to us (as is often the case with ancient non-European texts and artifacts, for instance, the *Gilgamesh* epic, already mired in textual problems), or is mysterious and elusive (which happens with many of our very contemporary third-world and post-colonial, post-modern artists and/or communities whose cultural identities, artifacts, concretions, and other non-homogenous, non-isochronic systems are to our eyes necessarily partial, distorted, biased and/or incomplete). The really complex point here is the following: if the utterance coming from the *other* is allegorical at a subterranean level, it means we must take a chance and risk interpreting it in view of *our own world, time and society* (not just the one in which the utterance first made its appearance, which historical exegesis and translation can more or less reliably reconstruct). This explains the many references in my work to the thought of Giambattista Vico, for whom allegory, in the form of myth and the fable, is a *vera narratio*,[5] a true (to the people who believe it and speak accordingly) description/ explanation, and enframing, of the world and its possible meanings. Vico, in fact, called allegory *diversiloquium*. (ib.)

This allegorical dimension is of course present in interpretive discourse as well–just think of the historical origins of criticism, of exegesis–and it would benefit both anthropology and hermeneutics if reflection is turned to the allegorical as the primal, originary, founding ability of language, as being context-bound and culture-specific. In this light, the critic becomes a story-teller, one who spins tales and is aware of the variety of reactions s/he may engender, whether political or sentimental, whether scientific or conversational.

❖

We must acknowledge that any approach to the outside world is effected

---

[4] This whether we follow Cassirer and the structuralists or side with the Dilthey-Gadamer tradition.
[5] Giambattista Vico, *The New Science of Giambattista Vico* (Ithaca: Cornell University Press, 1984) § 401, 403.

initially through our pre-conceptions and pre-judgments, those learned and habitual collective unconscious typologies that order somehow our existence. No need to summon Heidegger, Gadamer or cognitive psychologists on this fact. The point is not to stop there, but–and loosening a shaft for a recovery of phenomenology, in any of its developments–to allow this otherness, this not-readily understandable other-speech, to have its say, to be heard, to tell its story, and be considered *as such*. Again, this requires extended critical parsing of given frames of time in given places, spurring an on-going exchange *as if* between subjects (and not on the basis of a subject-object dichotomy), in an effort to describe successive levels of integration and relation, eventually attempt to formulate an evaluation and finally communicate it (we'll deal with this specific problem in a moment).

Two interpretive topics emerge at this juncture. At the metaphysical level, it means accepting a weak notion of ontology, for if we learned anything at all from Nietzsche, Heidegger, Derrida, Vattimo, Margolis, and Rorty, we must accept the notion of a *groundless being*, which is to say, that there is no grounding to existence other than what we ourselves construct and place there, and there is no supratemporal *arché* or divinity that stands as the ultimate axiom, other than the god(s) we invent in order to have some sort of frame of reference. But we should not panic. A thinking being is forever in motion, and although a *GeStell*, an enframing, is part and parcel of what language allows us to do (or is the only way in which it can come into existence), we also know, following Freud and the Existentialists, that what is needed is an *Entstellung*, a displacement, a dislocation of discourse, placing our very assumptions under alternative epistemological grids, that is, those *of* the others, the other members of the collectivity, exposing them to foreign eyes, so to speak. This is also consistent with Gianni Vattimo's elaboration of the notion of *Vervindung*,[6] which characterized all interpretation as intrinsically marked by *distortion*, as, at best, inevitable paraphrase and therefore possessing an added-sense, a variation, in short, a response (this I will claim is one of my ways of re-placing the politics of resistance). Under the sway of technology, having abandoned all pretense to totality or utopia, we should be more humble and ethically sensitive and, once again, accept full responsibility for the fact that during the

---

[6] Gianni Vattimo,"*Verwindung*: Nihilism and the Postmodern in Philosophy," *SubStance* 16.2 No. 53 (1987): 7-17. See also his *Le avventure della differenza* (Milano: Garzanti, 1980).

critical intervention, and especially when there is no common ground or shared code of values (as is the case when trying to make sense of experiences and texts from different sides of the boundary or separation line), there must exist a *spirit* of communication, a *concern* for the other (as not-me), and a *commitment* to seek a common ground for the exchange, even while we know that nothing is permanent.

At the critical level, it means that the methods we typically employ in sorting out what something new or alien or different means–whether through structuralist, marxist, post-colonialist, semiotic, or historicist approaches–should be considered as mere *propedeutic* procedure, as flexible and topical models, aimed not so much at finding the coherence of the *epistema*, of logical sense, as to just establish some background irrefutable *facts*, i.e.: uncontestable givens, such as: Napoleon died in 1821, he could not have participated in the Paris Commune, and so on too often the post-colonial critics are lacking in actual colonial history.

❖

A consequence of the above, at the rhetorical level, is that we must review carefully what takes place during a transaction between two individuals from radically different cultural backgrounds. First of all, does this guarantee us an "authentic," "true" interpretation? Not at all. In fact, it never does, as I just argued. Truth in interpretation is another overblown myth, for one could easily ask, and should ask, whose truth? The truth according to whom? Which forces and what laws and taboos are there in a given society which permit one articulation of discourse to be accepted as the truth, and another as heretical or subversive, or just plain unacceptable? Here, Michel Foucault is indispensable reading. The real concern in interpretation, as thus far elaborated, is *validity,* and with that *coherence with one's premises, rhetorical timeliness, ethical objectives.* I believe that, if the above requirements obtain, we are drawn somewhat "closer" to the *sense* of what we see (or hear). After all, who is the "real" American here amongst you? Identity politics is as ideological as its counterpart, difference and resistance politics. Can we not individually see how there are entire sectors of our being, which can be appropriated and manipulated by dominant forms of discourse in our own absolute present? It is not banal to recall, if we believe in literature, or claim to believe in literature, that we wear different masks and each audience recognizes only one or two among many to slip neatly in its own pre-established classificatory system. And it gets more complicated when this situation is retrojected back in time, for if you only think of your grandparents' parents, then you have already 16 diverse provenances each of which, of course, has experienced the same multiple-mask effect, being catalogued in entirely and possibly contradictory realms of discourse, social classes, symbolic universes. Who was the "real" Italian I encountered in 1973 in Bologna: the bourgeois landlady who preferred renting to an American instead of a Calabrian? the student who called me an American imperialist pig? or the professor who taught about the great writers of the second half of the XIX century in Marxist terms but never even once mentioned that soon after the new nation state come into existence nearly five million people left that country,–representing the greatest peacetime exodus in modern European history!–because there was no place for the great migration in the ideological and party driven agendas Marxists had in the late sixties/early seventies Italy?

All along, I have been making a case for the necessity of beginning with describing specific *place* and *situation;* for the need to take in as many lived aspects in as many given environments as possible *before* proceeding to rigorous analysis with clearly stated theories and methods. Moreover, in a frame of becoming, in a field of continuity, action can be preceded by meditation, by reflective consideration. The rhetorical act therefore must be understood as comprising several elements at once, or, better said, several *co-enabling vectors*. A speech is structured, it speaks of something outside of itself, it employs symbols and examples, and it is *directed at someone in a somewhere.* In this second phase of the rhetorical circuit, the interpreter may have to push the envelope of his/her recognizable sign- and symbol-systems, and try something else (which is more than just identifying and confirming), something other, in short, and create a sense, literally invent a meaning, attribute a value, tentatively, of course, but in the spirit of–and here is the crux!–a friendly encounter.

Even a brief exchange between two strangers requires some effort, capacity for risk, and a willingness to listen. I must now introduce other elements that go into the attempts at understanding. This includes at first the necessity of establishing, and relying on for any subsequent discourse, a *temporary yet co-validating social frame*, even when, indeed especially when, a concrete factual referntial situation is lacking. Consider it a hermeneutical suspended terrain of sorts. This is an in-between locus for the encounter, which has its own structure and can be called the horizon of comprehension. More than that, and coming back down to the world of *empiria*, to actual trans-national exchanges, whenever we meet the ethnographic text, the exile's discourse, or just plain foreign speech, meaning is obviously not readily available, is not said explicitly, or according to the grammars we know. It is therefore inevitably *transfigured*. Thus the exchange requires some imagination. It requires we appreciate historically denounced and disembodied rhetorical strategies as still enabling discursive patterns, as figures of thought, which have simultaneously a cognitive and ethical/political component.

At this level of analysis, the act of communication, the dialogue (whether critical or friendly and spontaneous) already manifests a cognitive element, it inscribes a knowledge no less valid than what we assume transpires in scientific exchanges. This is so because *rhetoric is actually the flip side of what we know as scientific method,* a structured moving machine that permitted the historic conquest and cataloguing of the cosmos.[7] Method and Theory are inextricably connected. Historically, Method won over Rhetoric, the seeds being already planted by Plato and the harvest cut and baled by Aristotle. But especially since Early Modern Times, valid knowledge could only be obtained through a codified and empowering methodology, the rhetorical progressively losing social credibility and political clout, not to mention intellectual respect. Yet what the ancient and medieval rhetoricians already knew, and what thinkers like Vico, Humboldt, Nietzsche, Kenneth Burke, and a few others developed, is the idea that *there is no such thing as unrhetorical speech.* In fact, besides their specialized knowledge, these theorists knew that any linguistic exchange is always enwrapped in some form of ideological power play. Hence the complexity of dealing with a foreign text or an alien interlocutor, where in an effort to decode, domesticate and catalogue, we often neglect that there is a power component at the source, and a power moment in the interpretation, in the appropriation and finally attribution of meaning to the

---

[7] See my two works on the relation between method and rhetoric, *Il fantasma di Hermes. Metodo, retorica, interpretare* (Lecce: Milella, 1996), and its augmented and rewritten version, *The Elusive Hermes. Method, Discourse, and the Critique of Interpretation* (Aurora, CO: The Davis Group Publishing, 2011).

original. And it contains also an ethical/political component because the articulation, now re-grounded upon what hermeneuticists call the *Lebenswelt*, the life-world, must needs a consciousness of the world-with-others. Notice that I have now introduced the next piece in the ontology of the rhetorical: language and thought are linked primordially, at the precategorical level. Language is the ether of co-existence, thinking is primarily a thinking *of the Other*, in metaphysical terms, and a thinking *of the others* in a postcolonial enframing. It should be manifest that in order to achieve this level of analysis I have had to recover the critical consciousness, and make recourse to a phenomenological method, as already hinted earlier.

Contrary to what a great part of twentieth-century linguistics has taught us–so wrapped up in showing how scientific, behavioristic, or logical it could be–the rhetorical exchange phenomenologically understood is the starting point for any philosophy, for any theory of knowledge, and is especially crucial in examining and evaluating ethnographic and migrant discourse.

Peter Carravetta
STONY BROOK UNIVERSITY

Abstraction and Materiality in Post-Holocaust Art
Colette Brunschwig's Collage Series *White Pebble for Paul Celan*

> the Jew and nature are two different things,
> still, even today, here too (Paul Celan).

Paul Celan (1920-1970)–originally Paul Ancel–was raised in Czernowitz, Rumania, in a German-language Jewish community. During World War II, he experienced forced ghettoization, suffered in a forced labor camp from 1942 to 1944, and lost his parents to deportations and death at the hands of the Nazis. From 1948 on, he lived in Paris, writing some nine volumes of poetry, translating from a wide variety of languages, and teaching German at the École normale supérieure. By the time he committed suicide in the Seine in 1970, having produced an œuvre widely recognized as the most important of any German language Jewish poet since World War II, Celan had become an important figure for a significant segment of the Parisian intellectual world, especially for its (sometimes only faintly still) Jewish artists, poets, and philosophers.[1]

Colette Brunschwig is a French Jewish "abstract" painter who currently lives and works in Paris. Born in Le Havre in 1927, but rooted further back in an Alsatian family–thus one on the linguistic-cultural border between Germany and France–she spent the last years of World War II in hiding, having fled after being betrayed to the Nazi occupiers by a classmate in the school she was attending in the South of France. After the War, she immersed herself in ancient and medieval Hebrew and Aramaic texts, and became a long-time friend of Emmanuel Lévinas (1905-1995), the Russian-French Jewish philosopher, whose thought she absorbed intensively although she took her distance,

---

[1] One index of this importance would be Emmanuel Levinas's essay, "Paul Celan/De l'être à l'autre," from 1972 (republished in Levinas 1976), but further indices are provided in the books on Celan by Jacques Derrida, Philippe Lacoue-Labarthe, and others.

as a painter, from his skepticism with respect to the aesthetic realm. In the nineteen eighties, thirty-some years into a painting career that had begun with, and continued to turn around, her dual struggle with the modernist "death" of representation and the felt impossibility of finding an adequate language in which to represent the extermination of European Jewry, Brunschwig undertook a series of collages based on the poetic works of Paul Celan, specifically *The Rose of No One*, a book that appeared in French translation in 1979. It is these collages that are the subject of the following remarks.

As Paul Celan was a poet for whom even Levinas was prepared to make an exception to his doubts about the aesthetic realm by stressing the ultra-ethical potential of Celan's poetry, Brunschwig had a particular reason, in her interest in Levinas's thought, to attempt to articulate her painterly thinking with Celan's poetic project. While Celan's works have been frequently set to music and used, or referred to, in the production of visual artworks, the collage series at stake here is plausibly situated in the context (among others) of, and in response to, the Levinasian reading of Celan.[2] But more broadly, the context in which it is necessary to see and read these collages is that of the tension between figuration and abstraction in modern art generally and post-Holocaust art specifically, so it is with a discussion of this complex and difficult context that I begin.

POST-HOLOCAUST ART BETWEEN FIGURATION AND ABSTRACTION

Discussions of the problem of artistic (and poetic) representation of the Holocaust turn largely around the vexed opposition between abstraction and figural (or realistic, representational) art.[3] The question of which of these sty-

---

[2] Levinas (1976) emphasizes in the Celan essay for example that Celan acknowledges a situation of a "langue pas pour toi et pas pour moi" (50)–for Celan, language cannot give us its presence–and that Celan sees the poem as a gift of this language to the other, a present marked by non-presence. By going beyond the dialectics of abstraction and referential realism, Celan is pushing into a realm that exceeds the desire for Heideggerian Being, a realm of the ethical service to the other. Brunschwig's collages attempt to serve the Celan poems precisely in the process of mourning we discuss below. – On other visual artists' projects that make prominent use of Celan, see Katz 2001, Martin 1983, Omer 1998, Reindl 1999, and Tan 2001.

[3] Primo Levi's critique of Celan's obscurity with respect to the problem of witnessing can be said to turn around this difference. In line with this critique at the realist, figurative extreme is Berel Lang's insistence that all representation has to be, in the last analysis, historical. Claude Lanzmann's denial that he is doing history in the *Shoah* film represents the opposite extreme, the rejection of the referential appeal. The

listic tendencies is to be preferred remains unresolved, despite the fact that artists are forced in practice to negotiate constantly some relationship to these opposed tendencies. For as I will argue here, a certain dialectic, or impossibility of choice, governs the relationship between figure and abstraction. On the one hand, if one fails to respond to the Holocaust in representational or figural terms, preferring abstraction, then one opens oneself to the objections or accusations of evasiveness, of a refusal of responsibility, of denial, of a flight into the aesthetic. On the other hand, if one presents all the horror of this history in figural (i.e. "realistically" representational) form, one opens oneself to the opposite criticisms: that one has aestheticized the terror of the Holocaust itself, that one has been insensitive to the viewer (and to the victims), and/or that one has hubristically claimed to reduce to a finite picture an evil and suffering the proportions of which are not measurable or masterable through finite depiction. (These alternatives in art and poetic writing that responds to the Holocaust are variants of the general dilemma faced by art in the modernist period, which presents itself as a choice between autonomous and engaged art, between subjectivism and objectivism, between expressionism and realism, and so on, depending on the specific context of discussion.) Both of these sets of reservations are plausible; each aesthetic alternative looks both good and bad in relation to the other one.[4] This makes it impossible to say in dogmatic, general terms what might make up an appropriate aesthetic response to the Holocaust.

In addition, from a Jewish perspective–in the sense of one that takes seriously and assumes a responsibility to adhere in some manner and degree to the Jewish tradition–the second commandment, forbidding the production of graven images, is both indeterminate as to its range–briefly: are all images forbidden, or just those that could be construed in idolatrous terms?–and counter-

---

question of abstraction vs. figurality within art overlaps, in turn, with the different question of whether or not art and fiction, or only history and nonfiction, can be adequate modalities of Holocaust representation.

[4] For texts that explore the questions of whether or not abstraction or realism in art is appropriate for Jewish communities and/or for Holocaust representation, see Amishai-Meisels 1993 (who sees abstraction psychologically as a self-distancing defense that, however, can in some cases be aesthetically and ethically justified with respect to post–Holocaust art), Kampf 1984, Pappas 2002, and Wong 1994.

balanced by another imperative to bear witness (Leviticus 5.1).[5] For a Jewish post-war European artist, especially one who has lived through the period of the Holocaust, the question will be double. First, how can one bear witness without producing (artistically, ethically, or religiously) illegitimate or objectionable images? And secondly, how can one question representation, and follow the questioning of representation that has already arisen out of the logical development of the arts in modernity toward modernist formalism–the notion of art as the self-reflection of art on its own possibilities–while at the same time responding–with acknowledgement, mourning, criticism, and appropriate horror–to a historical catastrophe that moreover itself arises out of an ideology (the National Socialist one) that is anti-modernist and anti-formalist (I return to this last point in a moment)?[6] This double question is the one consciously confronted, as I will show, by Celan and Brunschwig, the poet and artist who come together in the collages under consideration here. Each must represent history in some way, while acknowledging the impossibility of representation to be adequate to its object.[7] If in radical abstraction the concrete referent and its meaning tend to disappear into, or become effaced by, the signifying surface of the artwork's pure appearance, while the figurative impulse wants to make the work's surface subserve–and to the point of transparency–the objects portrayed (which would ultimately absorb in referential solidity their own sense), then the most advanced art in the post-Holocaust situation will have to explore the way in which these two extremes are dialectically involved with each other. For their artificial separation always involves the disavowal of one or more ineluctable dimensions of all semiological processes, as processes of never-ending mediation. There are infinitely many ways in which such an aesthetic exploration could be carried out (or could appear), of course, some of which would look more figurative, some more abstract, upon first view. The way in which Brunschwig carries out such an exploration in connection with Celan's

---

[5] See Lisa Saltzman (1999) for an unusually illuminating analysis of these matters in Adorno, Celan, and Kiefer with reference to the writings of Jean-Joseph Goux and Jean-François Lyotard.
[6] Granting the Nazis' selective acceptance of modern technology, which Jeffrey Herf (1984) importantly characterizes as their "reactionary modernism," I mean here "anti-modernism" in aesthetic terms, those of the Nazis' attack on "degenerate" art, to which we come in a moment.
[7] It is possible to interpret Celan in this direction when he says in "The Meridian" that we shouldn't think Mallarmé to the end.

poetry in her Celan-collages will be what I describe in the major part of this essay.

The Hostility of National Socialism to Representation as Obstacle to Presence

But first it is necessary to touch upon a point that is never, in my reading experience, brought out with sufficient clarity in discussions of the Holocaust and of its possible or impossible representation, however important and fruitful these discussions often are in other respects. While the history of the Nazis' exhibition and persecution of "degenerate art" is well-known, the relationships between the Nazi objection to such art and Nazi ideology in general, and more narrowly Nazi anti-Semitism, are not, I think, generally adequately grasped. Note that the majority of the works of "degenerate" art that the Nazis exhibit are neither purely abstract nor purely figurative. Instead, they involve what the Nazis consider distorted, atypical figuration, i.e. some complex mixture of figuration and abstraction whereby the two extreme tendencies co-exist in a dissonant harmony. What makes these works so objectionable from a Nazi point of view, then, is that abstraction and figuration commingle there without really fusing, as they do–ostensibly–in the neoclassical idealized realism of fascist Olympianism.[8] In other words, what the works of "degenerate" modernism suggest, insofar as we take them to constitute exemplary representations (or significant art), is that there is no representation without distortion, no figuration without the disruptive intervention of abstraction, and conversely no abstraction without representation (hence no spirit that is not dragged down by materiality, no origin that is not a repetition). What these works "re-present" to the fascists, then, is precisely *representation*, but representation insofar as it fails to represent, representation insofar as it fails to give us, and even renders impossible, immediate access to presence itself. And this notion–that humanity would not be able to get rid of representational processes and materials that fail to provide, and indeed interfere with, presence itself–is what Nazi ideology most needs and wants to disavow or deny. But where is it that

---

[8] Schuster (1987) provides an excellent and detailed overview of the "degenerate art" exhibits in connection with the establishment of the Nazi aesthetic in the art institutions of Germany during the late 30s.

we see this hostility to representation in Nazi ideology, beyond the condemnation of "degenerate" art? And how, more specifically, does their opposition to such representation organize, or structure, Nazi anti-Semitism itself?

The first of these questions is difficult to know how to answer briefly, but only because National Socialist ideology is everywhere and essentially directed toward the annihilation of representation in all its forms. What the National Socialists want in place of representation, as we have said, is simply presence itself, the immediate presence of the totality as such. (Hence, for example, the possibility of confusing, as Heidegger himself did for awhile, Heideggerian philosophy of Being with the National Socialist program.) Of course, *everyone* wants presence. Or at the very least, Western metaphysics in general is organized around the desire for presence, as Heidegger and, in a somewhat more skeptical or circumspect vein, also Derrida have both shown. Further, this metaphysics includes all views of representation that see the restoration of presence as representation's *raison d'être*. But the difference is this: in the Nazi ideology, the state–the "movement"–claims in racist terms to restore presence decisively and without recourse to the distorting and distancing mediations of representation. The presence sought and claimed by National Socialism is ostensibly embodied–to take a crucial and telling slogan as our example–in the unity of people, empire, and leader (*"ein Volk, ein Reich, ein Führer"*). This unity is considered a simultaneously natural and spiritual one–that of the Aryan race as principle of life. In service to this impossible ideal of pure presence–as fusion of people, state, and sovereign–the National Socialists must destroy and deny all representation. For representation–*semiosis*–always fails to provide us with full presence, which as such has to be that of both meaning and referent in a unity with the signifier or representative term. In place of immediacy, where there is representation one has mediation; in place of a home, dispersion; in place of nature, artifice; in place of essence, appearance; in place of unity, strewn multiplicity. A dispersed manifold of signifiers, distant referents, and uncertain meanings replaces the unity of Being. And this occurs on whatever level representation is engaged, from the distorted forms of modernist "degenerate" art mentioned above, which put a multiplicity of distorted perspectives and media in place of the natural wholeness of the healthy body, to the "eternal conversation" of parliamentary democracy, which according to Carl Schmitt, the "Crown Jurist" of the third Reich, delays and prevents forever the full self-presence of sovereign decision (Schmitt 1985).

Indeed, the Holocaust itself is both an effect and the essential core of the National Socialist total war on representation. The Nazis' racial anti-Semitism extends, displaces, and distorts a long tradition of Christian anti-Judaism that turns around the opposition between the "dead letter" of the Jewish law, on the one hand, and the "living spirit" of Christian faith.[9] In National Socialist ideology, although the Jews have become a race, and no longer merely the adherents of a religion, the connotations carried by this race are still largely those that had been carried by the Jewish religion from the standpoint of Christian discourse: the "dead letter"–language as death (or absence)–and "prefiguration"–rhetorical anticipation of the literal spirit of life that only Christianity, now "supplemented" by the Aryan race–can purvey.[10] The Jews have to be annihilated because they have been made to stand for, i.e. to represent, all that comes between the German collectivity and uninterrupted presence and self-presence, between the "movement" and vitality as "movement" itself. The Jews represent the barrier–otherwise known as language, and especially as writing, but sometimes also known as art, artifice, technique–between humanity and its own experience, the original and essential alienation of human nature from itself. From the Nazi point of view, it is a matter of life and death: to kill the Jews is to kill representation as death.

This barrier of deathly representation, however, has two aspects, which we need to distinguish before proceeding because they coincide with the two stylistic tendencies whose dialectic is at stake in Brunschwig and Celan. Namely, anti-Semitism views Jews as doubly noxious: by virtue of their excessively impersonal, anti-anthropomorphic and anti-natural monotheism, they are too *abstract*. God not only does not take the form of man in Judaism but is regarded therein as entirely non-representable. On the other hand, the Jews

---

[9] I have developed the history of relations between Christians and Jews in German culture from the late eighteenth century through modernism in terms of this tension between the "living spirit" and the "dead letter" in Librett 2000.

[10] I am invoking the notion of "supplement" developed at length by Jacques Derrida (1976) since *Of Grammatology* was first published in 1967.

appear to be bogged down in representations: the figures of law, ceremonial excesses, the bad literalism of circumcision, and so on. They seem overly *material*, as if they took images for things themselves. From this double point of view, then, the Jews stand at once for the idea that representation fails to achieve the presence it aims at, and for the idea that representations are all we have: they stand for the paradoxical impossibility and necessity of representation. At the same time, from the Christian point of view the Nazis inherit and displace, like "degenerate" artists the Jews in general fail to achieve any synthesis between an abstract spirit that cannot be made real and a figural reality–the opaque ceremonial law–that cannot be made ideal and that abandons the human world to an unredeemed condition. In contrast, Christianity claims to achieve this synthesis through Christ, while National Socialism claims to achieve it through the unity of signifying people, referential empire, and signified leader: *ein Volk, ein Reich, ein Führer*. Representation, then, as the rift between signified (God or Leader), signifier (law or Empire), and referent (the human world or People abandoned irredeemably in this rift), and as the necessity of the endless mediation between these terms, is "Jewish." Get rid of the Jews, according to Nazi anti-Semitism, and representation will give way to presence.

In light of this structure, any attempt to "represent" the Holocaust, or to "bear witness" to it, must bear witness also both to the unavoidable and profound limitations of representation, and to the role the disavowal of such representation played in the ideological–affective and conceptual–programming and carrying-out of the Holocaust by its perpetrators, and with the passive participation of its by-standers. How do Colette Brunschwig and Paul Celan wrestle with this task? How do they "represent" the Holocaust, while constantly "representing" not only the impossibility of adequately grasping or representing these excessively traumatic historical and individual events, but the impossibility and necessity of representation in general, the impossibility of constituting presence as such? As we shall see, it is by attempting to remain faithful to a certain abstract materiality or figurality of (and against) representation, one that has hybrid connections with both Judaism and the modernist and avant-garde art traditions (which are certainly not solely Judaic in their sources or motivating insights and experiences). Their works reflect incessantly on the undecidable tension between *abstraction* and *materiality* that both modernism and Judaism tend to stress, as I will show here with principal reference to Brunschwig's collages.

"WHITE PEBBLE FOR PAUL CELAN"–
COLETTE BRUNSCHWIG'S CELAN–COLLAGES

The Brunschwig collages I discuss here are works in ink and acrylic on paper and cardboard, in which Brunschwig has incorporated into the "images" the *proofs* for the French translation of Paul Celan's book, *The Rose of No One* (*La Rose de personne*), by Martine Broda. Thus, in one way or another the collages re-present Celan's poems and whatever it is that they in turn represent. As Brunschwig has written, the collages constitute–in addition to an homage and a statement of intellectual and artistic solidarity–an act of *mourning* for Celan in two senses. Brunschwig produced her collages as an act of mourning for Celan both in the sense of mourning his death, and in that of imaginatively helping him to complete the mourning for his parents and other lost ones. Hence, the title "White pebble for Paul Celan," that Brunschwig gave to the series when it was published as a book by Éditions Leo Scheer in 2001. For according to Jewish custom, mourners visiting the grave of a loved one place a small stone on the grave-marker. But the locution itself, "white pebble," comes from one of the poems worked into the collage series, "Siberian," which is one of the poems in which Celan in turn mourns the loss of Osip Mandelstam, to whom the collection, *The Rose of No One*, was dedicated. Celan also extensively translated Mandelstam's poetry, of course, including many poems from a volume entitled "The Stone." The phrase appears in the first of two stanzas I will quote from the middle of the poem (See Figure One):

> Little bell,
> left behind
> in the icy wind
> with your
> white pebble in your mouth:

> I too
> Have the thousand-year-colored
> Stone stuck in my throat, the heartstone,
> I too
> Am developing a patina
> On my lip.[11]

As these lines suggest, Brunschwig's title is taken from a figure in Celan for what enables and blocks–what makes possible, necessary, and at the same time impossible–a representation of the Holocaust. The "white pebble" is in a bell–enabling it to ring and/or preventing it from making any sound–and the bell is likened to a mouth, the mouth associated in turn with the poet's throat. The pebble becomes the stone of the traumatizing history of the Third Reich, the "thousand-year Empire." And the bell is abandoned, like the poet, in the deadly icy wind–a wind like that to which the slave laborers of the National Socialist "Empire" as well as the prisoners of the Gulag were exposed. The poet is like a statue, deadened and perhaps immortalized but nonetheless mortally subject to time, developing a patina. But further the patina here–"Grünspan" in German–recalls the name of the young Polish Jew–Herschel Grünspan–whose shooting of the German Secretary in the Germany embassy in Paris, Ernst vom Rath, on November 7, 1938 the Nazis used as a pretext for launching *Kristallnacht*, which signaled the turn toward the explicit politics of extermination. The white pebble is thus also a "stone of the heart"–*Herzstein*–weighing the poet down into a silencing sadness. But at the same time, the pebble in the mouth recalls the pebbles Demosthenes is reported to have held in his mouth, in order to overcome a speech impediment, when he practiced declaiming on long walks. As we cannot trace here, this imagery of stone–grave-stones, stones slaves labored to extract from the earth, the stone Moses struck, etc.–proliferates throughout *The Rose of No One* and beyond, across Celan's *œuvre*. For Brunschwig, it is to be heard as an echo of the Hebrew root, *dalet mem mem*, which joins the Hebrew words for silence, grave, stone, and whispering, and

---

[11] "Kleine, im Eiswind/liegengebliebene/Schelle/mit deinem/weissen Kiesel im Mund.//Auch mir/steht der tausendjahrfarbene/Stein in der Kehle, der Herzstein,/auch ich/setze Grünspan an/an der Lippe."

includes homonymic, if not also etymological echoes of the words for blood and for tears.

But if the collages thus both attempt to mourn for Celan and to represent the problematic of (impossible, but necessary) representation that he represents, why the formal medium of *collage* itself? What does the form "collage" here represent? First, and on the one hand, Brunschwig's conception is linked by resemblance to Celan's works in that she–and this quite plausibly–regards Celan's style as collage-like: he breaks words into fragments of syllables and letters, and he uses new compounds to exploit the resources of the German language (e.g. "tausendjahrfarben" and "Herzstein" in the part of *Sibirian* quoted above). In this way, he both highlights and resists the destructive negativity through which the language, as he puts it, has passed. Further, in line

---

[12] Photos of Brunschwig collages by Richard Gehrke, collections photographer, Jordan Schnitzer Museum of Art, University of Oregon.

with the surrealist influences that are also associated with collage, he often combines jarringly disparate images and contexts.

On the other hand, precisely because collage is an art-form that is constructed through metonymic figures and differential juxtapositions, even more than by likenesses, what Brunschwig's collages are "like" here, is poems that are not "like" themselves. In this way, for example, the representativity of the collages vis-à-vis the poems ironizes itself. Further, the collages here incorporate what they mourn, rather than imitating it–the poems become a *piece* of the collages, not exactly a likeness, or if so, an internally disjointed one. In turn, the collage-form also affirms Brunschwig, rather than Celan, as subject of this art, in that it incorporates by its very name the name of the artist–Col-lette. In a further reflexion and deflexion, this piece of the artist's name recalls three Hebrew homonyms–the words for "voice" and for "all"–*kol* (קוֹל) and *kol* (כל) in two different spellings–which recall the voice and totality of the people, Israel, but also the word for "completion, destruction, and annihilation," kala (כָּ֗לָ֗א). Totalizing recollection of a lost presence is here marked by the incompleteness with which completion strikes itself, at least traditionally, in the wake of the second Temple's destruction.

Before considering the visual qualities of the collages themselves, we have to consider one more preliminary question: what are the collages working with or on? The collages incorporate and attempt to mourn not just Celan or his poetry in general but specifically "proofs"–*épreuves*–of a translation. As the page-proofs constitute an "original reproduction," like the first print of a photograph, Brunschwig is at once acknowledging the de-auraticization of the work of art in the age of mechanical reproduction and resisting it, by turning the proofs into an "original" work of art. Her intuition seems to be that if mechanical reproduction is taken to rid art of all subjective singularity, then it risks disavowing the difficulties and complexities of representation by denying the existence of meaning or sense pure and simple, such that only reference would remain.[13] But "épreuves" are not just "page-proofs" but also "ordeals,

---

[13] Brunschwig lays out this position in "Résistance de la peinture." Cf. Celan's remarks on "Dichtung" as "das schicksalhaft Einmalige der Sprache" (III, 175), which suggests an auratic view that he however complicates by going on to say: "Noch im Hier und Jetzt des Gedichts–das Gedicht selbst hat ja immer nur diese eine, einmalige, punktuelle Gegenwart–, noch in dieser Unmittelbarkeit und Nähe läßt es das ihm, dem Anderen,

trials" and as such Brunschwig is treating here both Celan's ordeals in general and his specific ordeals of being-in-translation, the multiplicity of languages and arts, of idioms and styles, that make representation, as reconstitution of full presence, an enduring impossibility and infinite task. As Jacques Derrida has persuasively argued, with respect to Celan especially in "Poetics and Politics of Witnessing" and "Majesties" (both essays in Derrida 2005), "witnessing" involves a performative relationship of fidelity to truth in the absence of calculatively guaranteed "proof." This is why witnessing can and must involve an assumption of responsibility for the truth of a representation that is always subject to doubt. To a striking degree in accordance with such a notion of witnessing, Brunschwig here bears witness to an *épreuve sans preuve*, the undergoing of an uncertain translation of experience under Babelian conditions. In this context, we should recall Primo Levi's multiple characterizations of the concentration-camps as a Babelian world (Levi 1996). In short, it is not just that there was an ordeal of the Holocaust and then a separate ordeal of the attempt to represent or translate that experience. Rather, the ordeal of the Holocaust involved a suffering under the multiplicity of languages–not understanding orders in camps, for example, could be deadly–a suffering thus tied to the Nazi attempt to efface all language as such by reducing it to the one language of the Aryan race as embodied in the Leader's words.

So if the collages bear witness to the Holocaust as works of mourning for the proofs of impossible translation, then how do they visually and conceptually structure this witness in relation to what we can now call their "prooftexts"? Most generally, and like all of Brunschwig's work, the collages belong to postwar "abstract" modernism.[14] They represent no objects or people in any obvious way, but explore elementary forms–circles, ellipses, squares, rectangles–and develop textures, light, depths, and traces, in an art of suggestion and nuance, framing and counterframing, effacing and reinscription, in accordance

---

Eigenste mitsprechen: dessen Zeit" (III, 199). Here, the temporality of the other co-constitutes the "immediacy" of the poem.

[14] For work that has interestingly complicated our understanding of post-War abstraction in America in relation to the largely repressed or denied Jewish ethnic backgrounds of several of its key practitioners and in relation to the Holocaust, see Baigell 2002, Godfrey 2003 and 2004, and Wolff 2003. On the vicissitudes of abstraction and figurative art in post-War France, see Wilson 1993, Ragon 1988, and Kelly 1997.

with a sensitivity to the continuity of writing and painting that Brunschwig discovered early in her career in Chinese calligraphy. Brunschwig's art develops a quasi-Kantian transcendental analysis of the possibility- and impossibility-conditions of representation. But in this analysis, the difference between transcendental logic and transcendental aesthetics, of conceptual frames and sensuous images, becomes undecidable. In the context of the verbal texts, however, which although not simply mimetic or expressive point to or evoke objects, actions, subjects, body-parts, events, perceptions, and significations, Brunschwig's shapes and textured traits seem to hint sometimes at the figural representation of things mentioned in the poems. They do not entirely cease to "stand for," even if *what* they "stand for" is never quite determinable, and even if what they "stand for" always includes the impossibility, as well as the necessity, of "standing for" or "pointing to."[15] In this way, while not figural, they place themselves beyond the ideology of pure abstraction characteristic of, say, abstract expressionist modernism in the criticism of Clement Greenberg and Michael Fried.[16]

For the remainder of this essay, I would like to demonstrate Brunschwig's position between abstraction and figuralism by focussing specifically on one formal aspect, namely the way in which Brunschwig insistently puts to work and unsettles within the collage itself the opposition between *frame* and *image*. If a framing device, a framework or frame of reference, supplies the abstraction—like a code—in terms of which an image takes on meaning, in turn an image provides a material illustration or instantiation of the framing code, the interpretive framework. The harmonious *synthesis* of abstract framework (or background) and material image (or foreground), of "prefiguration" and "fulfillment," is required for there to be a concrete totality of presence, as was formulated in philosophical aesthetics, for example, from Schiller to Hegel, culminating in the latter's definition of "beauty" as "sensuous shining of the

---

[15] Consider the Celan-poem called "Standing," from the collection that followed *The Rose of No One*, and that is amongst those poems that have been set by Wolfgang Rihm: "Stehen im Schatten/des Wundenmals in der Luft.//Für-niemand-und-nichts-Stehn./Unerkannt,/für dich/allein.//Mit allem, was darin Raum hat,/auch ohne/Sprache."

[16] One might even suggest that the linkage with Celan's text functions to ensure for Brunschwig's abstract *œuvre* that it be understood in reference to the Holocaust.

Idea." But it is precisely this totality that Brunschwig's collages–mourning the proofs of (Celan's) translation–refuse to provide, or attempt to recall that they cannot provide. Abstraction and materiality remain separate, even if they also cross into and interfere with each other repeatedly.

Consider the way the collages break down, in terms of their design, into a typology of forms, discrete groups.

1. A first group comprises a rectangular frame, generally higher than it is wide, containing frames within it, in a doorlike or windowlike pattern, where the text is situated within the interior frame or frames in one or both languages. This group is exemplified in the collages based on the poems entitled "Bei Tag," "Nachmittag," and "Was geschah?" (See Figure Two [for "Was geschah?"].)

2. A second series comprises gridlike frameworks (recalling among other things *Sprachgitter*, the title of the Celan-book prior to *Die Niemandsrose*) with four main sections, sometimes subdivided, in which pieces of text and circles or

ellipses (originally circumscribing the figure of "globes" from the first poem) are framed. Here the frame expands to fill the entire area of the image; it multiplies itself into a grid.[17] This series comprises "Les globes," "Mandorla" "Chymisch II" (which appears as a "detail"), "Envoi I" (another "detail" view of this pattern), "Psalm," and "Die hellen Steine." (See Figure Three [for ""Les globes"].)

3. Third, as was the case with the "Siberian" image considered above, a tall, whitish-gray rectangular column (usually containing text), stands against an unframed background of black, or perhaps a rectangular opening penetrates

---

[17] Rosalind Krauss's ("Grids" in Krauss 1985) incisive analysis of the duplicities of the "grid" in modernist painting–as spirit and matter, as a figure for both the autonomy of art and its inscription in history–illustrates with respect to the "grid" the general interplay between abstraction and materiality I am suggesting characterizes both Brunschwig's and Celan's works. Whereas Krauss begins by stressing that the modernist "grid" was largely successful in "walling the visual arts into a realm of exclusive visuality and defending them against the intrusion of speech" (9), it is striking that Brunschwig's grids here precisely *articulate* word with image. The Celan-collages, and her work more generally, do not fit easily within the ideology of modernist abstraction.

a wall of black. The uncertainties about figure and ground, opening and closure, raise in visual form uncertainties about presence and absence (and representation) more generally. In each case, the image, which has no strong framing gestures within itself, is accompanied by another column or strip of light, and perhaps a third figure, a circle or a third, sketchy piece of light. Variations on this pattern govern a number of other images in the series, including "Sibirisch," "Schwarzerde," "Chymisch I," and "Hawdalah." Here, the absence of strong framing gestures is striking, as if the image had to do without frame, even as background and foreground are made, to some extent, difficult to determine or ambiguous. To the extent that the main "figural" features in these visual textures are rectangles, it is as if they consisted essentially of broken-off pieces of the frameworks depicted in the first and second types of collage-structures outlined above. The instance of the code is here a piece of the code.

4. Finally, there are images that we would have difficulty assimilating to any of these patterns, as they combine elements of each and drift away from all. In so doing, they prompt us to ask in a new way if generalization or abstraction is possible at all, or if rather all is radical dispersion, infinite particularity. But these collages themselves continue to create forms and to allude to patterns established by their contexts: they insist on the possibility of general meaning. Examples of these collages that adhere to none of the previous three patterns are the collages built around the poems, "Mit allen Gedanken," "Erratisch," "Envoi II," "Mit allen Gedanken," and "Le Menhir." (See Figure Four [for "Erratic"].) In "Erratic," we have the two circles and framing rectangles from the quadratured images, the second series, but the quadrature or grid is lacking and the rectangles recall the columns of light we were just looking at, as they have moved more toward the center of the image. In "Mit allen Gedanken," the quadratures of circles and text with gridlike framing are present, as well as, in the center on the bottom half of the image, the kind of door-like frame we had at the center of the first group of images I mentioned. "Envoi" fits only with difficulty into any of the patterns established in the other images, although it maintains a loose relation to the third pattern of a black ground with a white rectangle of light and one or two other whiter patches or images.

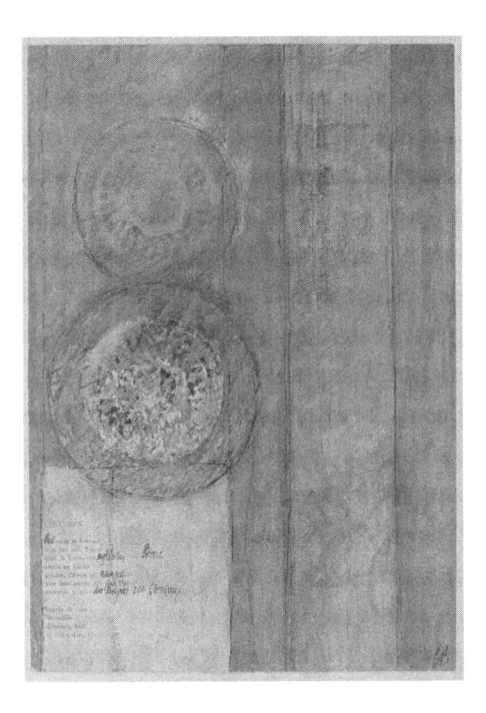

Finally, "Le Menhir" (See Figure Five [for "Le Menhir"]), which concludes the series as Brunschwig sequenced it in *Caillou blanc pour Paul Celan*, participates in both the framing grid pattern (pattern two) and the pattern based on a main column of light (pattern three), but here it is the *dark* column that is between two *lighter* ones. It seems here that image (or figure) and frame (or abstraction) entirely coincide: the image is a frame, the frame an image, grid and column at once. Yet the foreground/background relations do not cease to be ambiguous, in the relations between the three main vertical rectangles. There seems to be a depth behind or within the tableau while at the same time the surface-strokes insist on the radical superficiality of their traces. Further, patches of underlying, unpainted surface remain uncovered, most visibly in the upper right. This undercuts the stasis and balance achieved in the final image, by suggesting its partiality, its non-totality. A support appears, but it is a support that unsettles the integrity of the work, its autonomous unity. The coalescence of image and frame, figure and ground, is thus incomplete, just as their synthesis will always reappear as an annihilation of either image or frame, figure or ground, excessively material (and imaginary) or excessively abstract (and cerebral). Appropriately, this final image of the series incorporates and effaces a poem in which an abstract idol is addressed as God qua "abyss of heaven."

The last word, then, is the ongoing reversal obsessively recurrent in Celan: the inversion of above and below, heaven and abyss, abstract universal God and material nothingness. The tension between these two extremes of representation—abstract idea and material image—which interfere with and replace each other without a stop, appears before the "abyss of heaven" as the "gray shape" that, in Celan's poem, steps forth onto "dark" and "white-meadow paths." Brunschwig's collages, and her brushes, will have attempted to explore these paths, in their search for an articulation of overwhelming collective loss with the renewed insistence on the significance found in giving up both oneself and one's art in the name of the other.

Jeffrey S. Librett
University of Oregon

LITERATURE CITED

Amishai-Maisels, Ziva. 1993. *Depiction and Interpretation: the Influence of the Holocaust on the Visual Arts*. Oxford: Pergamon.

Baigell, Matthew. 2002. *Jewish Artists in New York*. New Brunswick and London: Rutgers University Press.

Brunschwig, Colette. 2003. "Résistances de la peinture." *Colette Brunschwig en andere transposities van de poëzie van Paul Celan/et autre résonances autour de l'oeuvre poétique de Paul Celan*, ed. Etty Mulder and Daan Van Speybroeck. Netherlands, Nijmegen University Press.

———. 2001. *Caillou Blanc pour Paul Celan*. Paris: Léo Scheer.

Derrida, Jacques. 1976. *Of Grammatology*. Baltimore: Johns Hopkins University Press.

———. 2005. *Sovereignties in Question: the Poetics of Paul Celan*, ed. Thomas Dutoit and Outi Pasanen. New York: Fordham University Press.

Godfrey, Mark. 2003. "Burnt Books and Absent Meaning: Morris Louis's *Charred Journal: Firewritten* Series and the Holocaust." *Image and Remembrance: Representation and the Holocaust*, ed. Shelley Hornstein and Florence Jacobowitz, 175-200. Bloomington: Indiana University Press.

———. 2004. "Barnett Newman's Stations and the Memory of the Holocaust." *October* 108: 35-50.

Kampf, Avram. 1984. *Jewish Experience in the Art of the Twentieth-Century*. South Hadley, MA: Bergin and Garvey Publishers.

Katz, Michele. 2001. "L'image en ses limites: le travail des traces an art plastique." *Verso* 23: 26-9.

Kelly, Debra. 1997. "Loss and Recuperation, Order and Subversion: Post-War Painting in France 1945-51." *French Cultural Studies* 8.22: 53-66.

Krauss, Rosalind E. 1985. *The Originality of the Avant-Garde and Other Modernist Myths*. Cambridge, MA and London: MIT Press.

Levi, Primo. 1996. *Survival in Auschwitz: the Nazi Assault on Humanity*. New York: Simon and Schuster.

Levinas, Emmanuel. 1976. *Noms propres*. Paris: Fata Morgana.

Librett, Jeffrey. 2000. *The Rhetoric of Cultural Dialogue: Jews and Germans from Moses Mendelssohn to Richard Wagner and Beyond*. Stanford: Stanford U Press.

Martin, Rupert. 1983. "Anselm Kiefer." *Artscribe* 43: 26-30.

Omer, Mordechai. 1998. "'As One Speaks to Stone': the Evocation of Celan's Poetry in the Works of Micha Ullman and Adam Berg." *Assaph. Studies in Art History* 3: 287-300.

Pappas, Andrea. 2002. "The Picture at Menorah Journal: Making 'Jewish Art'." *American Jewish History* 90.3: 205-38.

Ragon, Michel. 1988. "The Return of Abstraction." *Cimaise* 35.195-196: 17-24.

Raphael, Melissa. 2006. "The Mystery of the Slashed Nose and the Empty Box." *Journal of Modern Jewish Studies* 5.1: 1-19.

Reindl, Uta. M. 1999. "Belu-Simion Fainaru: BAIT/HAUS." *Kunstforum International* 143: 376-7.

Saltzman, Lisa. 1999. "To Figure or Not to Figure: the Iconoclastic Proscription and its Theoretical Legacy." *Jewish Identity in Modern Art*, ed. Catherine M. Soussloff, 67-84. Berkeley: University of California Press.

Schmitt, Carl. 1985. *Politische Theologie. Vier Kapitel zur Lehre von der Souveränität. Vierte Auflage.* Berlin: Duncker and Humblot. Schuster, Peter-Klaus, ed. 1987. *Nationalsozialismus und >Entartete Kunst<. Die >Kunststadt< München 1937.* Munich: Prestel Verlag.

Tan, Eugene. 2001. "Jane Bustin." *Art Review* 53: 49.

Wilson, Sarah. 1993. "Paris Post-War: in Search of the Absolute." *Paris Post-War: Art and Existentialism 1945-55*, 25-52, ed. Frances Morris. London: Tate Gallery.

Wolff, Janet. 2003. "The Iconic and the Allusive: the Case for Beauty in Post-Holocaust Art." *Image and Remembrance: Representation and the Holocaust*, ed. Shelley Hornstein and Florence Jacobowitz, 153-74. Bloomington: Indiana U Press.

Wong, Janay Jadine. 1994. "Synagogue Art of the 1950s: a New Context for Abstraction." *Art Journal* 53.4: 37-43.

Diaspora and Identity in Latin American Jewish Writing

The Jewish Diaspora placed Jews in virtually every corner of the world. Several factors make these diverse groups of Jews "one" group. To begin with, religion is one of the strongest ties connecting Jews everywhere. Many Jews however, are not religious. The sharing of a common past and destiny– that of the biblical narratives and all the history that followed, the persecutions, the frustrated tentative of so many empires to subjugate and eliminate them, the Inquisition, and the pogroms, composes an unconscious part of Jewish identity. All these calamities and persecutions helped to strengthen Jewish identity. The topic of identity is highly debated among Jewish scholars as well as a recurrent theme in works of literature written by Jewish authors throughout the world. In the twentieth century, several historical events such as the Holocaust and the formation of the State of Israel in 1948 have shaped and transformed the way Jewish people regard themselves. Latin America has seen its waves of Jewish immigration from colonial times throughout the twentieth century. This hybrid and complex blend has produced a number of Latin American Jewish writers who discuss the topic of identity in their novels, revealing not only questions regarding their Jewishness, but also of their situation as a minority in Latin American societies.

In my study I consider aspects of memory, identity, and assimilation, and observe how the characters of the novels under discussion relate to their local communities, how they deal with their exile, with their conflicts of identity, and ultimately, how the characters reflect the writers' own reality. Benedict Anderson emphasizes how aware we are about the contingency of our origins, our genetic heritage, our gender, our life-era, our physical capabilities, our mother-tongue and so forth (10). We are born under a series of unavoidable circumstances that escape our control. Anderson talks about the concept of "imagined communities" where individuals are connected to an imaginary community of habits, traditions, languages, culture, etc. That is how Chinese, Jamaicans, Cubans, Portuguese, everywhere in the world, create in their surrounding environment, elements that make them feel closer to "home." They may be living hundreds of miles away from their original lands, but they are able to recreate a space, a neighborhood, where they feel connected. Anderson explains that "religious communities" kept people connected by sacred texts and religious practices that made them one group. With the decline of ancient religious communities, languages, and lineages along history, other changes took place in apprehending the world, which made it possible to create the idea of "nation." For Jews all over the world, a Jewish nation did not exist until 1948, their nation had to be an "imagined nation," a promised land kept in their hearts and faithfully waited for.

Back in 2004 the magazine *Psychology Today* had an article entitled "The Identity Dance," in which the author interviews identical twins to find out what similarities and differences there are among them. The article suggests that although "genes [may] influence character and personality more than anything else does," things are not as simple as they seem. Identical twins with identical genes can, in fact, be very different people. Not only "genes" "determine identity" (53). This "rigid idea," the article continues, "has been replaced with a more flexible and complex view in which DNA and life experience conspire to mold our personalities" (57).

Ian Craibs, in his book *Experiencing Identity*, comments that the "central feature of the self in modern society is its reflexivity, a constant questioning and reconstruction of the self in a lifetime project. "We are constantly constructing and revising our personal stories and so reconstructing our selves" (2). Identity is an ongoing process of modifying ourselves, and is never stagnant and never completely finished. Diana Fuss adds something interesting to this idea of "constructing our selves"; she argues that "experience is not merely constructed" but it is also constructing itself (25). Our ever-changing identities are thus a result of many combined elements: genes, DNA, life experience, and the influence of the societies in which we live. It is after all, a process in which we are constantly reviewing and reconstructing who we are.

In order to explore the question of Jewish identity I am going to comment on the work of some Latin American Jewish authors, whose fictional characters represent the qualities and struggles of real Jewish individuals. No matter where they come from, their identity will be impacted by the local culture as well as the Judaic code of behavior and beliefs inherited from their ancestry. How they assume or hide their original identity, and how they resist or give in to assimilation varies on many different levels.

Before I move on to the Latin American writers who are the focus of this study, I want to comment on a novel by a Nobel Prize winning author, Isaac Bashevis Singer (1902-1991), and his book *Enemies, A Love Story*. The main protagonist is a tormented Holocaust survivor, Herman, living in New York in the years after the Holocaust.[1] Herman survives the Holocaust thanks to a gentile Polish peasant who hides him in a hayloft at her home. After the war, he marries her in gratitude and comes to America. Herman lives a constant turmoil, an endless pain of doubt and sorrow. He constantly questions his Jewishness:

> Refugees from Germany strolled by [...]. They were talking about houses, shops, the stock market. 'In what way are they my brothers and sisters?' Herman asked himself. 'What does their Jewishness consist of? What is my Jewishness?' They all had the same wish: to assimilate as quickly as possible and get rid of their accents. Herman belonged neither to them nor to the American, Polish, or Russian Jews. (114)

His behavior indicates the abyss of his life: "Herman fasted but did not go to the synagogue. He couldn't bring himself to be like one of those assimilated Jews who only prayed on the High Holy Days. He sometimes prayed to God when he was not fighting with Him [...]" (147). Throughout the narrative, we learn that Yadwiga, the gentile he married, loves Herman and decides to convert to Judaism. For him, Judaism in America is the following: "The neighbors were waiting for Yadwiga downstairs, eager to include her in their circle, to teach her the Judaism that remained from their mothers and grandmothers

---

[1] Isaac Bashevis Singer, born in 1904 in Radzymin, Poland, died in 1991 in the United States. In 1978 he received the Nobel Prize for Literature.

and which the years in America had diluted and distorted" (148). Herman doesn't feel like "those assimilated Jews" and thinks that Judaism in America is "diluted and distorted." Herman–a fictitious character–gives voice to the thoughts of real Jewish individuals who, similarly tormented, ask themselves questions about their own identity and religiosity.

In the Argentinean novel "No tan distinto" by Marcelo Birmajer (1966-), the Argentinean Jew Saúl Bluman travels to Israel looking for answers regarding his identity. Saúl wishes to know if he is a good Jew. The book narrates his encounter with relatives and strangers in Israel, with the religion that he never practiced, and finally with himself. The important aspect about the several encounters that Saúl has with other Jews throughout the narrative is that each individual Jew, is Jewish in his or her own way, but none seems to have the answers to the questions that he makes along the way. Saúl travels out of his Jewish neighborhood, the Once, in Buenos Aires to the land of Israel, hoping to find peace of mind and hoping he will find that he is as Jewish as everybody else. His contact with the great diversity of Jewish individuals along the novel, from Buenos Aires to Israel, and from Israel to the orthodox Jews of Cuba, bring him to realize that they are all Jews, in different ways, in different degrees of religiosity and assimilation, each one adopting the Jewishness that seems more suitable for their beliefs and life styles.

The devastation of assimilation and change in identity is not always directly depicted. In the short story "Uncle Facundo" by Argentinean Isidoro Blaisten (1933-2004), the happy domestic life of a Jewish family in Buenos Aires is gradually changed by the unexpected visit of Uncle Facundo, a mysterious relative whose behavior and way of being affects all those around him. The balanced and functional family of four reluctantly embraces the uncle who slowly changes each and every one of them, turning the house into chaos. Little by little, the members of the family start dropping their dearest moral principals by adopting the corruptive immoral behavior of Uncle Facundo. Decadence is inevitable until, one by one; they are convinced they have to kill Uncle Facundo in order to restore the life they had previously. Every member of the family participates in the assassination of the undesirable uncle who is buried inside one of the walls of the house. Here, assimilation is seen as a threatening, invisible force that drags the whole family into an abyss of corruption. At the end, the family seems to go back to their old routine and only a nebulous memory of Uncle Facundo stays in the back of their minds. Their lives are back to normal but they will never be the same.

Margo Glantz (1930-), a Mexican-born Jewish writer, explores her family history in her novel "Genealogies" (1981) where she retells the stories of her parents' past. Glantz unfolds some of the most crucial as well as ordinary moments of the lives of these immigrants from Russia and Eastern Europe who found in Mexico a home not always so welcoming to Jews. The detailed, sometimes tragic stories of the pogroms experienced by the family are told by her mother and then by her father and it is Glants who comments: "Living with someone probably means losing part of your own identity. Living with someone contaminates; my father alters my mother's childhood and she loses her patience listening to some accounts of my father's childhood" (181). The stories told happened more than fifty years ago and it all seems distant from her mothers' eyes now. The past is a mixture of confusing memories from both her parents. They seem not to be individuals, but one. Their past history makes them one person, with one same past connecting them.

Nelson Vieira, professor at Brown University has recently published a book on three Brazilian Jewish authors who are viewed as "outsiders within" the Brazilian culture. They are: Clarice Lispector (1920-1977), Samuel Rawet (1929-1984) and Moacyr Scliar (1937-). Clarice Lispector was born in the Ukraine and got to Brazil when she was only two months old. Her family spoke Yiddish at home but not much is known of her Jewish background. That aspect of her identity, her Jewishness, was something that most people ignored. Lispector's writing doesn't refer in any instance to her origins. It is simply not there. However, the total absence of her Jewish identity in her writing speaks louder than most texts by other authors who directly talk about their identity. Her most common topics deal with our deepest fears, our hidden emotions, and the turmoil of every day life. In her own words in an interview, Lispector describes her writing as chaotic, intense, out of reality.[2] Her writing is dense,

---

[2] Interview available on www.youtube.com, under the title "Entrevista Clarice Lispector." Journalist Julio Lerner interviewed Clarice Lispector in 1977 for the tv show Panorama.

hermetic, sometimes hard to decipher. In 1971, the collection of short stories entitled "Felicidade Clandestina"[3] that includes the famous short story "O Ovo e a Galinha"[4] was written based on the impact of the death of a criminal, Mineirinho, assassinated by the police with thirteen bullets in Rio de Janeiro. In an interview given before her death in 1977, Lispector explains that the way in which Mineirinho was killed caused her great revulsion: "one bullet was enough" she says, "the rest was just haughtiness." In the short story that she wrote about Mineirinho, she describes how each one of the thirteen bullets affects her in a different way. The last bullet turns the narrator into the victim himself, he personifies Mineirinho's pain. In the interview she doesn't smile, but she explains that "today, I am sad, because I am tired" and later she clarifies, "I am tired of myself."

Readers can find Lispector's Jewishness in the great ability she had on showing human despair, in describing the most painful fears of often innocent and marginalized characters. The silence regarding her identity could have very well been an invisible shield of protection that Lispector chose for herself. Theorist Fredrik Barth explains that "Since belonging to an ethnic category implies being a certain kind of person, having that basic identity; it also implies a claim to be judged, and to judge oneself, by those standards that are relevant to that identity" (14). Lispector hated labels, she didn't even like to be considered a writer. Ignoring her Jewish identity protected her literature and herself from being judged and classified under the labels she so much despised. Another interesting aspect about the author's life is that she was married to a Brazilian diplomat and went to live in Europe with him during World War II. Her Jewish origin was protected by her husband's profession and social status. I wonder how she might have felt at the knowledge of the events of the Holocaust. She was in Europe in the years that followed the war and as a writer and a journalist she was probably very aware of the news that unraveled after the investigations regarding the Nazi persecution to Jews. She never made any comments regarding this time.

---

[3] *Covert Joy* (1971).
[4] *The Egg and the Chicken*, my translation.

Samuel Rawet was born in Poland and went to Brazil at the age of seven. He wrote stories about immigrants who can't manage to fit in, individuals who fell displaced, uneasy, and uncomfortable. He spoke Portuguese like a native speaker and was a brilliant engineer. His short stories depict characters haunted by invisible fears of insecurity, inferiority and loneliness. The author wishes to make the reader think, he challenges the reader to penetrate a world of internal conflict and feelings of inadequacy. He was an introverted man who, in the later years of his life, adopted some strange behavior: he would walk down the streets of Brasilia wearing shorts and flip-flops, holding a bird cage in his hand. When asked what the bird cage was for, he would reply: "I am going to catch Jewish rats."[5] Rawet felt the stigma of his Jewish ancestry and didn't know how to get rid of it. In his literature we verify that there is great internal tension between his identity defined by his family history and the desire to disengage himself from the idea of the "persecuted–victimized–Jew." He wrote a series of short stories that reveal the need for self-annihilation, to escape the discrete violence of everyday life, the wounding pain of innocent prejudice and the sarcasm revealed in people's conversations.

Author Susana Gertopan (1956-), born in Asuncion, Paraguay, wrote a novel entitled "Barrio Palestina" (1998) where the narrator is a boy–Móishele –who tells the story of how his family had to leave Poland right before the German occupation. Móishele describes the feelings they had as they arrived in the tropical land of Paraguay, to live in a type of Jewish ghetto where people from Vilna, Warsaw and other Polish cities already were. The occupants of Barrio Palestina spoke Yiddish and fought to make a living and to adapt to the new circumstances. At the time of their departure the family has no idea of the horrendous events that would take place during the war and the mass extermination of Jews. Móishele talks about the difficulties encountered by the family in this primitive and rural region of Paraguay: the hot weather, the anger, the wish to return as soon as possible. The reader watches how resistant his mother is to settling down in this strange land. She profoundly dislikes the neighborhood, the climate, and the new conditions of her life. Móishele observes how his mother kept all the family's clothes inside their suitcases for

---

[5] Renard Perez. http://www.anenet.com.br/biografias_relacao.htm. "Biografias in memoriam," Feb 5, 2008.

more than a year. It is only when they start receiving letters from relatives who remained in Europe and realize the persecution and the danger of certain death that they have escaped, that she slowly empties the suitcases and organizes the clothes in the closets. Here a different form of resistance, in the behavior of a mother who cannot accept having left her country, is revealed in the simple act of keeping the suitcases ready for departure, ready to return home. The mother's resistance slowly fades away and the family settles down. One of the most positive aspects that this forced exile represents to Móishele is the great feeling of freedom that he can now enjoy, so different from the atmosphere of their home town when pogroms put their lives in danger: "Me era difícil creer que podíamos caminar tranquilos y libres, sin miedo" (108) and "(…) pero lo mejor era que podía caminar libre y sin temores, caminar por barrio Palestina, llegar hasta el mercado, y también hasta el puerto, ya conocía el camino, y estaba seguro que no me perdería" (110). Not only physical freedom is deeply appreciated but also the freedom to choose what to do and where to go. At the end of the book, Móishele is a young man who moves to Israel since the ideal of Zionism never died inside himself. He explains: "Dentro de mí bullía el sentimiento judío, ese sentimiento que no permitía el olvido, esa fuerza que nos mantuvo vivos, y con la mente lúcida para recordar" (180).

I have explored different degrees of Jewishness in the characters of the novels discussed as well as the authors themselves. The study of these representations may provide more understanding on how kaleidoscopic these characters are. The "Jewish individual" cannot be defined but he or she can be better understood, and better perceived by readers, be they Jewish or non-Jewish. Identity is influenced by memory, by different degrees of assimilation determined by life experience that is happening every day, with every human contact. It is an on-going process where the individual's identity is never completely finished. Jews all over the world are connected by an imaginary community where shared beliefs, behavior, tradition, religion has bound them together throughout the centuries. Recently, as I talked to a Jewish-Argentinean friend, she mentioned a popular saying that expresses the idea of Jewish continuity: "los nietos quieren recordar lo que los padres quisieron olvidar," which reflects well what the young generations of Jewish Latin American authors are doing:

trying to remember and register those things that their grandparents wanted to forget. The need to remember the past and pass it to the younger generations makes possible the transmission of myths, traditions, and values that are fundamental for the continuity of these communities even if assimilation and adaptation occurs. The essence always remains.[6]

Debora Cordeiro Rosa
University of Central Florida

Works Cited

Anderson, Benedict. Imagined Communities. London: Verso, 1983.

Birmajer, Marcelo. No tan distinto. Buenos Aires: Grupo Editorial Norma, 2000.

Blaisten, Isidoro. "El tío Facundo." Cuentos anteriores. Buenos Aires: Ediciones de Belgrano, 1984.

Craibs, Ian. Experiencing Identity. London: SAGE, 1998.

Gertopan, Susana. Barrio Palestina. Asunción: Arandurā Editorial, 1998.

Glantz, Margo. Las genealogías. Mexico City: Martín Casillas, 1981.

Lispector, Clarice. Felicidade clandestina. Rio de Janeiro: Nova Fronteira, 1981.

Singer, Isaac Bashevis. Enemies, A Love Story. New York: Farrar, Straus and Giroux, 1972.

Sinha, Gunjan. "The Identity Dance." Psychology Today. Mar-Apr. 2004. 52-62.

Vieira, Nelson. Jewish Voices in Brazilian Literature: A Prophetic Discourse of Alterity. Gainesville: U P Florida, 1995.

---

[6] After the formation of the Jewish State in 1948, the situation of exile and Diaspora for Jews all over the world has changed. However, for those who continue in the Diaspora, a sort of "portable promised land" is carried inside every Jewish individual. They are able to adapt and blossom in any community, since they have a shelter in the imaginary community–the invisible link–that connects Jews from everywhere.

Three Waves of Immigration
Waving (Wavene) the Flag of Patriotic Fervor

Much has been written about the Cuban diaspora, its reasons for exile, its means of exile, the differences among members of the diaspora, and the expectations of the exile community to return to Cuba. Now that some exiles have spent the majority of their lives in the United States while watching friends and family die–nearly a quarter of a million Cubans have died here since the first wave arrived in 1959–we have to consider the consequences, or the legacy of this exile. Primarily, we have first generation exiles who were adults when they came here, the 1.5 generation that came here as children and have matured within the confines of the United States, and now their children and grandchildren who have only known life in the United States. The result is that often not only do two different cultures clash, but also several different generations within one culture, as Henry Pérez and Mary S. Vásquez have noted. Nevertheless, Gustavo Pérez-Firmat points out in *Life on the Hyphen* that "Although it is true enough that the 1.5 generation is 'marginal' to both its native and its adopted cultures, the inverse may be equally accurate: only the 1.5 generation is marginal to *neither* culture" (4). This salient observation proves true on both levels even though the 1.5 generation is a rickety bridge between the other two generations that is about to collapse as identification with Cuba sways toward identification with America and finally implodes into identification with the South in particular for some writers.

I have detailed the moribund nature of Cuban culture in the U. S. in a previous article on *Raining Backwards* (Deaver). In that article, I stated that something new arises as each culture affects the other and transculturation occurs. Roberto G. Fernández details the disappearance of Cuba as a focal point in his *oeuvre*. While Miami's Cuban enclave is the setting for his early works, his later works move toward a more regional setting that is virtually devoid of references to Cuba and the cultural clash. For instance, Isabel Alvarez-Borland believes:

> Throughout these narratives, the author maintains implicitly that community can come only from the recognition of difference. For Fernández, the future of the Cuban community in the United States can progress only by ongoing negotiations between Cuban and American communities since each has something the other needs in order to survive. (106)

This comment ties into Pérez-Firmat's ideas regarding the marginal nature of the 1.5 generation, or its inverse, the sense of belonging to both cultures. I propose that even among the 1.5 generation, the members feel more at home here than they would in Cuba. One only need consider that Pérez-Firmat himself has written *Carolina Cuban*, privileging Carolina over Cuba. Why not Cuban Tarheel or Cuban Carolinian? Fernández, like Pérez-Firmat, moves toward this apparent assimilation in one of his most recent short stories, "Is in the Stars (for Lisa Photos)," which on the surface has nothing to do with Cuba, but rather depicts Southern culture on the skids whose death throes, like those of Cuban culture within the borders of the U. S., seem interminable–yet weaker and weaker. Hence, one legacy of exile is the loss/gain or rejection/acceptance of cultural identity, or the constant struggle between the two for some sort of equilibrium. This is what Pérez-Firmat, in pugilistic terms, calls "un clinch" (2000 11) even though this term could also signify to win decisively or to embrace passionately rather than engage in a stalemate in which neither side gains superiority.

While Fernández's early works were published in Spanish, he has recently enjoyed great success and critical acclaim with his English efforts. Why the move from Spanish to English? Alvarez-Borland provides the response:

> In a panel discussion on Cuban-American literature held in Orlando, Florida, in 1996, author Roberto Fernández was asked by a member of the audience why he had decided to publish his last two novels in English. He replied, "I write in English so that the future generations of Cubans in the U.S. can read me." In my mind, what Roberto Fernández said had to do with his intense

need to know that if his literature was not going to be part of Cuban letters, his work had to survive somehow for the community that will always live abroad. (154)

Let me emphasize the end of that last sentence: "the community that will always live abroad." An exile, purportedly would want to return to the country of origin. In this citation, we see a writer and a critic who have fatalistically admitted that they are here to stay despite any notions held by the first generation. The exile is approaching its fiftieth year in some cases and the resignation evident in Fernández's unstated rejection as a Cuban artist signals that his audience will be a monolingual American community at worst, or a functionally illiterate group of Spanish-language heritage speakers at best. Since that article, Fernández has had works that appeared in Cuban collections though, which could make it difficult to categorize his work in the future. Does he belong to the canon of U. S. ethnic writers or can Cuba claim him as a writer who falls under the rubric of Latin American literature? Unlike Dorothy in the <u>Wizard of Oz</u>, he cannot click his heels and say, "There's no place like home" to return to the land of Ostracism, where he would be considered a *gusano*.

In other words, he has the freedom and mobility to transcend borders from the American side of the hyphen. He has turned a negative into a positive. Consequently, exile has given way to nationalization and a new sense of patriotic duty. This Cuban-American writer begins to shift focus from Cuba to America, but without ignoring the Cuban heritage. Alvarez-Borland posits, "Exile has indeed proved to be a positive experience for the members of the second generation as the physical distance from their original geography and culture has led these writers to look anew at the values and traditions of Cuban culture" (156). Cuba is no longer home–rather, it is a distant memory–and you cannot go home again. Humberto López-Cruz seems to agree, at least in the case of Fernández. He opines, "El discurso humorístico de *Raining Backwards* no sugiere la continuidad cultural que puede esperarse con el transcurso de las generaciones; la ruptura es abrupta y la resistencia a la asimilación fracasa" (19). Conversely, Virgil Suárez and Delia Poey proffer that, "Cuban-Americans are not assimilated; they do not adopt the dominant culture, but rather adapt it. Thus, Cuban-American writers use English, stretching, bending and playing with it, to accommodate their needs–doing whatever it takes to keep the language vibrant and vital, on their own terms" (11). Suárez and Poey make an interesting observation here that is true to a point. Cuban-Americans do adapt the culture, but I believe they are assimilated.

Consider that besides Fernández and Pérez-Firmat, Achy Obejas, Virgil Suárez, Elías Miguel Muñoz, Cristina García, and Oscar Hijuelos write in English. Hijuelos is the most accessible and recognizable of these writers to an English only audience, but all of them show control of the language and customs in the U. S. On the other hand, Mayra Montero, a Cuban writer living in Puerto Rico, persistently writes in Spanish and does not figure into exile literature anthologies for the most part. She does fall under the category of Latin American literature however. Unlike the other authors mentioned, she has not assimilated and seems recalcitrant to do so. She is the exception to the rule of assimilation and has preferred to live within the confines of yet another island, the other wing of the same bird, with the only real difference being that Puerto Rico has a unique status as a U. S. territory that enjoys the privilege of democracy to a degree.

First, Puerto Ricans are U. S. citizens, but they pay no federal income tax. Corporations located on the island do not pay federal income tax on their earnings either. How much does Ron Bacardí (the patriarch is buried in Santa Ifigenia cemetery in Cuba) earn each year? Puerto Ricans do not need a passport to travel between the island and the mainland. They are eligible for federal benefits, but subject to conscription; however, they may not vote in federal elections unless they live on the mainland. They have a representative in Congress, but the electee cannot vote on legislation. Cuban-Americans, on the other hand, are politically active and several representatives at the federal level come from their ranks. On a final note, Puerto Rico has its own U. S. subsidized Olympic team. I can think of no other ethnic group that has this exclusive benefit; consequently, not all Hispanics enjoy the same privileges. The wet foot/dry foot policy toward Cuban refugees attests to this notion when compared to the policies enforced against Mexican border crossers. This is another legacy of Cuban exiles: they are welcomed as political refugees when they touch dry land, but Mexicans face imminent deportation if they cross the border since we do not have a wet back/dry back policy. In essence, Cuban-Americans are able to enjoy a fully integrated sense of citizenship when compared to some of the other Hispanic groups in the United States.

Returning to Fernández, I think that he has overcome the tendency to depict a cultural clash between ethnic groups, but this remains to be seen in his future works. On the other hand, Pérez-Firmat states, "Someone like Fernández writes what might be termed anglophobic English, a Spanish-English hybrid or 'Spanglish' that endeavors to make itself unintelligible to people who don't speak Spanish to begin with. He doesn't say, 'Let me out!'–but rather, 'I'm not leaving!'" (1994, 145). This was true in *Raining Backwards* (1988), but less so in *Holy Radishes!* (1995). In his most recent short stories, I think the Spanglish is noticeably absent and I fail to see the use of anglophobic English in them.

This transition, in part, is attributable to the expansion of Fernández's audience from the Cuban-American community in Miami to the world at large. He has moved from satirizing the monolingual or the inept bilingual to lampooning Southern culture since it is not a big step from the plantation heritage of the Southern Pearl of the Antilles to that of Dixie. As proof of the focus on Miami in the earlier works, we need only to consult Pérez-Firmat, who contends that, "Miami Spanish includes a term that, so far as I know, is unique to the city of sun and solecisms: *nilingüe*. Just as a *bilingüe* is someone who speaks two languages, (say, Spanish and English), a *nilingüe* is someone who doesn't speak either: 'ni español, ni inglés.' Such a person is a no-linguist, a nulli-glot" (1994, 46). Now, as a Virginian, I have seen the northern bias toward my southern accent and have been told that I speak a substandard dialect of English (at the University of Washington in 1987) as well as by a public speaking professor from New York (Manuela Reynolds) at the University of Virginia around 1979-80. In fact, Professor Reynolds told our class that she loathed a Southern accent and would take points off of our speeches if we did not make an effort to speak correct English. At Florida State University, someone told me that I had a country accent. Evidently, Southerners and Cuban-Americans suffer from the same problem regarding what is perceived as standard English;

hence we can draw a parallel between the two cultures and the notion of ni-lingüismo. This is another legacy of exile: loss of first language ability while learning a second language or the lack of mastery in either language. Pérez-Firmat has pointed out in *Life on the Hyphen* that this is the particular affliction of Desi Arnaz. On the other hand, the diligent can master both languages through education, as we see in various Cuban-American authors.

Like Cuban-Americans, Southerners have suffered a form of ostracism because of their linguistic idiosyncracies. The difference is that after our own Civil War (a Northern term that implies one union) or the War between the States (a Southern term that suggests two different countries), the South was invaded by carpetbaggers and we are still in a stage of economic and cultural recovery nearly one hundred fifty years later after a scorched earth policy that destroyed nearly everything in our region. Like the Cubans in Miami, we struggle with a past that haunts us, whose legacy is with us and hanging on, but on the brink of vanishing. We need only consider the recent upheavals and protests regarding the Confederate battle flag that appeared as part of various Southern state flags and the removal of that emblem after referendums. Georgia removed the image. African-Americans boycotted South Carolina for refusing to stop flying the Confederate flag at the state capitol. Virginia slyly incorporated Martin Luther King Day, a federally mandated holiday, as part of Lee-Jackson Day, a state holiday, which now bears the name Lee-Jackson-King Day. When Richmond erected a statue in honor of Arthur Ashe, it fueled controversy because his statue is on Monument Avenue, which is lined with commemorations to Confederate heroes. On one hand, we could perceive Virginia's acts as inclusive and healing–especially if we consider that one of the mainstays of the Confederacy is the only state to elect an African-American governor, Douglas Wilder. On the other hand, it may be outright defiance and a tenacious effort to preserve states' rights and autonomy as well as tradition.

This in your face defiance is what Pérez-Firmat describes as the third stage of exile experience, even though Southerners are not in exile, but rather an apparent state of military occupation. He says, "Destitution gives way to institution, to the establishment of a new relation between person and place. To institute is to stand one's ground, to dig in and endure. Thus, the theme of the third stage is not 'we are there' or 'we are nowhere,' but rather, 'here we are'" (1994, 11). The parallel between the Southerners and Cuban-Americans is stronger when we consider Pérez-Firmat's comments beside the last words of Faulkner's *The Sound and the Fury*, which was first published in 1929, a scant 64 years after America's War between the States, "They endured" (Faulkner 427). The CSA lost the war and despite Northern efforts to make us assimilate, we still take pride in the best traditions of the South. Like some Cuban-Americans, some Southerners refuse to let all the traditions die even though the effort may now be effete. Perhaps this is why 89 out of 201 U. S. military bases are located in the 13 states that comprised the Confederacy. The remaining 112 bases are dispersed throughout the other 37 states. That's roughly an average of seven bases per Southern state; three per the rest of the nation. Could this be a vestige of Reconstruction and the fear that the South will rise again? Or is it for national defense to protect our coastlines? One only need look at the attack on the Pentagon on September 11, 2001 to dispel that notion. By the same token, the U. S. has had a navy fueling station at Guantánamo Bay since 1903. In both cases, the idea of "Yankee Go Home" arises even though Yankee has a different connotation for a Southerner and a Cuban.

I have made this point because the flag and language are depicted as central to preserving Southern culture and Cuban-American culture since both cultures are intertwined in terms of plantation society with its notions of genteel society, a similar lack of language prestige perceived by other speakers of their respective languages, a related history of slavery, a comparable climate, and a futile yet patriotic fervor in retaining the memory if not the tangible aspects of a people that had to start anew in the wake of losing nearly all their property. Regarding Cuban-Americans, Pérez-Firmat acknowledges:

> The painful knowledge that they live in exile has been attenuated by the comforting feeling that they never left. You walk into a restaurant on Eighth Street and not only does it have the same name as one in Cuba, but it probably has a map of Havana on the wall and a Cuban flag over the counter. You *know* you're in Miami, but still you *feel* at home. (1994, 10)

The same is true for Southerners. We are proud to be Americans, but we only feel at home in Dixie; hence, the popular bumper sticker "American by Birth/Southern by the Grace of God." While I deplore displaying the Confederate flag as a sign of racial hatred and its appropriation by bigots, hate mongers, and White Supremacists, I have no qualms about seeing one that is flown as a sense of cultural pride in honor of ancestors who lost their possessions and died to be free defending their principles and autonomy. Unfortunately, many people now associate that flag with bigotry, ignorance, and the redneck way of life. Still, I am prouder to be a Southerner than to be an American. To me, the food is better here, the language is richer with its many nuances and dialects, the culture is familiar, the people are friendlier, and the history has personal meaning. You know you are in the South when you see the flag on the wall or on the back of a pick-up. I go to Chicago, New York, or out West and I'm in my country, but I'm not at home until I get back in the South where everything is much slower, relaxed, and people wave their hands, not necessarily the flag.

The flag is a symbol that recurs in nearly all of Fernández's major works. This symbol has been explored by various critics, but the image has changed from the Cuban flag to the Confederate battle flag. For instance, Linda Lucía, the girl flag appears in at least four of Fernández's works with minor changes in the first three cases, and a major change in the last one. In *La vida es un special*, Linda Lucía makes her first appearance. She is the dehumanized, girl-flag whose body has been dyed to resemble the Cuban flag, which is now personified through her. The dye fades, but has left an indelible cultural mark on her. Metaphorically, this suggests that you cannot deny your heritage. It is imprinted forever; hence, an immigrant may believe that he/she is 100% American, but one's true colors will always show. Linda Lucía says, "Fíjese bien en mi piel. Tiene franjas azules y blancas. Y yo no soy zebra. . . . Fíjese bien que son azules y blancas. Las zebras son negras y blancas. Por favor, dígame que no soy zebra, dígame que soy bandera, aunque me encadenen de nuevo" (Fernández 1981, 52). Unlike the popular anti-terrorist, pro-war sticker prevalent today, these colors do run or bleed. Linda Lucía would rather be objectified rather than animalized in her dehumanization, even though she fails to understand the importance of the flag's symbolism.

Linda Lucía appears again in *La montaña rusa*, where she does not understand why she is turned into a human flag. Here, she reveals, "... y me dijo que me pondrían una estrella en la frente y franjas por el cuerpo y me asusté y le pregunté el significado de todo aquello y no me supo contestar, sólo que así lo habían dejado escrito los viejos" (Fernández 1985 36). Tradition supersedes understanding here since the old ones have decreed that it be done. The flag has lost meaning to her parents and to her. History has transformed into her story, without rhyme or reason, since the flag holds no meaning to her. Her mother merely wants to win a competition rather than celebrate the heritage that the flag should represent. Rather than preserve the culture, it symbolizes a state of oblivion and her personal martyrdom has nothing in common with the collective martyrdom of the first generation of exiles. The flag dyes her and dies on her. This is yet another legacy of exile: history loses its immediacy and sense of urgency.

In *Raining Backwards*, Linda Lucía describes the same event in English, "'... and they told me they would put a star on my forehead and stripes on my body and I got scared and asked them the meaning of all that, and they didn't know how to answer, they could only say they were obeying sacred traditions'" (Fernández 1988, 219). The obvious change is the language shift from Spanish to English in this depiction, but the subtle changes are the ambiguous shift from the third person singular to the third person plural in terms of subject/verb agreement, and the move from the writings of the elders to sacred traditions. In this case, anonymity is the key now that the elders are unnamed and converted into traditions to be followed while losing the importance of the tradition itself.

Earlier in the same novel, an announcement is made, "Don't forget our annual fraternity dinner on September 24. Linda Lucia, living symbol of our fatherland, has accepted our invitation and she will be honoring us with her presence" (Fernández 1988, 34). Two things are noteworthy here. First, is it a coincidence that September 24 is Fernández's birthday? Second, does the link between annual fraternity dinner and September 24 with a Cuban flag in attendance suggest that your birth occurs only once and you never lose the connection to your place of birth? I think so. Once again, I will emphasize that even though I now live in Georgia, and have for the last fourteen years, that I am a Virginian, not a Georgian–despite what my driver's license stipulates as my state of residency.

In a similar vein, Pérez-Firmat ends his *Cincuenta lecciones de exilio y desexilio*, one lesson to represent each year of the fifty years that he had completed at the time, thusly, "En el comedor, mis hijos, pacientes. . .han estado esperando que termine de escribir. Al verme llegar, cantan en coro: "–¡Apio verde to you, Papi!" (2000, 123). In this instance, he appears to hear the English "Happy Birthday" in Spanish as what would be translated as "Green Celery to you, Papi." Originally, I thought that this suggests that even though he has an excellent command of English, when he is thinking in Spanish, that is what he hears when someone else speaks to him in English; however, Gustavo pointed out at this symposium that it is a parody he learned in Cuba as a child. Like Linda Lucía, the marks of Cuba are a stigmata that appear on him, but he understands the reasons why and negotiates both languages and cultures even though at times it discomfits him. Cuba and Spanish are permanently etched on this 1.5 generation even though neither may form part of its children's lives. I see this same struggle with my own children who understand Spanish, but refuse to speak it–except haltingly and in staccato bursts to their Peruvian grandparents. For the most part, they prefer to eat chicken nuggets and pizza rather than typical Peruvian food. They would be hard pressed to describe the Peruvian flag.

Raining Backwards begins and ends with the idea of the flag. At the beginning, Fernández parodies a bumper sticker that could be seen in Miami in the eighties, "WILL THE LAST AMERICAN TO LEAVE MIAMI PLEASE BRING THE FLAG" (1988 9). At the midpoint of the novel, he demonstrates that the influx of Spanish- and French-speaking immigrants from the Caribbean and Central America to Miami have now become Americans as the phrase becomes, "WILL EL LAST AMERICANO TO LEAVE MIAMI S'IL VOU [sic] PLAIT BRING THE BANDERA" (1988 111). Since these pleas are in capital letters, we have to question the idea of majority/minority cultures which leads us to conclude that the majority is now multi-ethnic, multi-racial, and multi-lingual. Or perhaps, nulli-glot and incapable of speaking any one language. Finally, the novel ends with John F. Kennedy's promise at the Orange Bowl to a Cuban audience that, "I CAN ASSURE YOU THAT THIS FLAG WILL BE RETURNED IN A FREE HAVANA" (1988 223). Gabriella Ibieta believes that:

> Framed as it is by these two statements, the text becomes a commentary not only on the Cuban exiles and their Cuban-American children, but also on their cultural and political context in the United States. The first statement, referring as it does to the American flag, is a biting comment on the "invasion" of South Florida not only by Cubans, but also by Haitians, Nicaraguans and other Latin-Americans.... The second statement, alluding to the Cuban flag, is in a sense parallel to the first statement. Taken out of context, Kennedy's words, referring to a flag that will never be returned to the Havana that the pro-Batista Cubans knew, sound particularly ironic. This statement, then, like the first one, also denies history and its consequences. (69-70)

Of course, Havana is not free and the flag has not been returned. In fact, Ibieta stresses that veterans of the brigade in attendance at the Kennedy speech had to hire a lawyer in 1976 to petition for the return of the flag to them from storage at the Massachusetts home of the Kennedy library where it rested in a box. It is poignant that a box, in Spanish "una caja," is a synonym for a coffin.

Another critic, Guillermo B. Irizarry, analyzes the importance of the flag in *Raining Backwards*. He writes:

> The novel also makes light of patriotic fervor, of anticommunism and of the love for the Cuban national flag. The character of the flag-girl is the vehicle for a biting critique of patriotism. Linda Lucía, whose name is a pun on a popular song about the flag looking pretty–in Spanish, *linda lucía* carries the stigma and suffering of patriotic fervor on her own body.... Linda Lucía and her imaginative story line become an eerie reminder of the extremes of patriotism. The vehicle of parody gives a comedic charge to this tragic story and follows through with our author's literary project. (597)

Purportedly, according to Irizarry, this literary project is "...the difficult and improbable function of serving as a translation from Spanish to English, and from Cuba to the United States. In this sense his narrative attempts to serve as a bridge between cultures, languages, histories, and nations" (591). A bridge suggests bi-directionality, but the Cuban-Americans who have come here cannot go back. Pérez-Firmat confirms this idea when he philosophizes, "Lección del exilio: el único regreso posible es hacia adentro, no hacia atrás" (2000 51). If that is the case, when one looks inward, which is a space in itself, the searcher must move forward; consequently, introspection takes precedence over retrospection–yet another legacy of exile: the ontological quest.

Linda Lucía and the Cuban flag fall into oblivion by the time Fernández writes "Is in the Stars (For Lisa Photos)." Here, the country singer Amber Marie bears the marks of the Confederate battle flag. Just as in Linda Lucía's case, her mother dyed her to win a competition. She says, "'My whole body was crimson, and then she painted two blue bars that went from my right foot to my left shoulder and from my right shoulder to my left foot. The two bars intercepted right at my belly button. . . . Then she took white shoe polish and painted stars inside the bars'" (Fernández 2001, 65). Perhaps living in Tallahassee and teaching in Alabama have forced Fernández to reconcile himself to the fact that he is a Southerner now. In fact, he is included in *Race Mixing: Southern Fiction since the Sixties* (2004) by Suzanne W. Jones as well as in *Southern Writers: A New Biographical Dictionary* (2006) by Joseph M. Flora, Amber Vogel, and Bryan Albin Giemza. Virgil Suárez and Gustavo Pérez-Firmat also appear in the latter work. This problematizes the categorization of these writers even more if we think strictly in terms of exclusivity. On the other hand, if they are marginal to neither group–Cuban or American--they have achieved acceptance into both groups and easily erase the border suggested by the hyphen. The question remains whether this idea of inclusion is a mere convenience for publishing and selling books, or an actual feeling of belonging.

Traditions die hard in the South. I know from my days at Florida State University that Tallahassee celebrates Old South Day, reminiscent of *Gone with the Wind*, when fraternity and sorority members at FSU garb themselves in period dress while parading through town. The Florida state flag bears the bars that are a reminder of the Confederate flag although the stars do not appear on the bars. The title of the short story under study has a structure that suggests Spanish syntax rather than English and appears to be a calque of "Está en las estrellas" since the subject pronoun is omitted in English. Furthermore, two other references suggest a link to Cuba. First, we see a veiled remark that hints at Operation Peter Pan when Amber Marie says:

> Mama, in her rage, put me on a Greyhound with a note attached to me. The note had the address of some old cousins of Meemaw that had moved to Philadelphia. When the driver of the bus took me there and they saw me all painted like that, they said they didn't want no trouble with their neighbors. The following day they took me to the welfare office and from then on I went from foster home to foster home until Mamma Loi took me in. Mamma Loi was an old lady from Port-au-Prince who nourished my soul and patiently scrubbed me with mangrove extract to remove the red and blue color from my skin. The stars were a different story. But, I got accustomed to them. She told me. 'Don't worry about the stars, child. If they don't fade it's because you're destined to shine like them.' And here I am today. (Fernández 2001, 65)

This familial abandonment is reminiscent of numerous Cuban children sent here alone during the 1960s. Oddly, the people of the City of Brotherly Love display callous indifference to Amber Marie's plight because of her Southern characteristics, however implausible the situation may seem regarding her physical appearance (her *parecer* and her *aparecer*) in Philadelphia. The other reference to Cuba is in the deformation of Mamma Loi, a character who helps the rebellious slave Mackandal in Alejo Carpentier's *El reino de este mundo*, into Mamma Loi, who helps and consoles a White girl considered to be anathema by her family. Moreover, Mamma Loi foretells Amber Marie's future success, which hints at Santería.

Nevertheless, the historical reality is much more in line with Southern attitudes and the setting is completely out of the rural South:

> The afternoon of the contest, I sat on top of a bale of hay on the bed of Mr. Olsen's pick up [sic] truck. I waved to the crowds with my chained hands. Behind me there was a big sign that said: *Yankees Go Home*! I was paraded up and down Main Street, and the loudspeakers mounted on top of the pick-up

blared the cotton song. (65)

Here, Amber has no idea that "Dixie" is the actual name of the cotton song, even though she is a country singer who should know the title since many country bars play "Dixie" as the signal that the bar is closed. History is denied in this case as the younger generation of Southerners apparently have no recollection of their past and like Linda Lucía, merely follow traditions without understanding why the traditions arose in the first place. Furthermore, the command "Yankees Go Home!" recalls the bumper sticker parodied in *Raining Backwards*, "WILL THE LAST AMERICAN TO LEAVE MIAMI PLEASE BRING THE FLAG." The difference here is that now the plea of surrender to a foreign invasion has become an imperative to preserve a culture that wants to oust a culture that is perceived as foreign. In other words, the xenophobic attitude toward speakers of other languages in *Raining Backwards* is transformed into an anti-imperialistic response to an invasion of Northerners that speak the same language, but whose accent and customs are different and unwelcome. Once again, Yankee is a signifier with different signifieds when used by a Cuban (all Americans) and by a Southerner (strictly Northerners), but the significance is one of anti-intervention.

Just as Linda Lucía's mother pandered her for profit at Cuban-American functions, Amber Marie's mother follows suit in a Southern context. Amber Marie says:

> Mama was so sure I was going to win the contest, becoming the official flag, that she had already rented me out for different community events like the Jackson Peanut Festival, Jefferson Davis's Birthday, the Watermelon Festival, PTA meetings, the Secessionist Movement rally, and the annual meeting of the Daughters of the Society for the Return of the Good Ole Society. (65)

The parody of the wistful longing for something that will never come about is evident in the potpourri of inane festivals yoked to ardent Southern partisan political associations. Since Fernández is Cuban-American, this might be viewed as offensive stereotyping. On the other hand, he may consider himself as a Southerner now, which makes the parody more acceptable. This seems the more logical conclusion if we believe that he has now crossed the bridge from Cuban to Southern American. In "Transcending the Culture of Exile: *Raining Backwards*," Gabriella Ibieta states:

> In fact, if Fernández were not Cuban-American himself, his portrayal of Cuban Miami might be interpreted as offensive and stereotyped. But followed as it is by President Kennedy's promise ("I can assure you that this flag will be returned in a free Havana") as the book's closing words, Fernández' [sic] ironic message becomes decipherable: Mima and her Cuban-American children, as well as the Cuban exiles that they exemplify, have become a genuine part of American culture, even while retaining some vestiges of "Cubanness." We are all here to stay. (74)

The vestiges of Cubanness are apparent in the title of the short story under consideration. That "we are all here to stay" is evident in the shift from Cuban culture to Southern culture and the penchant to maintain a heritage that will never return. Nonetheless, the Cuban accent is present in this work given that the girl-flag has appeared in all of the other works mentioned and that the flag will continue to have some sort of meaning as long as someone is waving it.

Southern culture endures just as Cuban-American culture endures. For instance, Tom Petty, who hails from Gainesville, Florida has made a Rock and Roll Hall of Fame career with numerous hits. Two of his albums are entitled *Southern Accents* (1985, which contains the songs "Rebels" and "Southern Accents") and *Pack up the Plantation* (1991, live recordings while on tour). The titles alone suggest that like Cuban-Americans, Southerners refuse to assimilate completely. As Virgil Suárez noted, we adapt the culture to our own ends. My theory is that the 1.5 generation has lived here so long that they will always have their Cuban accents, just as Southerners will also be marked by their accents. The rest of America will judge us and them based on these traits. The North will continue to exert its influence on exterminating these cultural markers while preaching diversity yet practicing discrimination because it won the war. Our children will prefer to assimilate toward mainstream models in order to avoid any sort of difference. As Petty sings in "Southern Accents," "There's a Southern accent, where I come from, the young uns call it country, the yankees call it dumb. . ." (Petty). Once again, this ties into Pérez-Firmat's notions about a nulli-glot, while at the same time privileging one dialect over another as even our children forsake a traditional cultural marker.

To me, it is not a far leap for a Cuban-American living in Florida to consider himself a Southerner. For Cuban-Americans, Castro is not a hero, but rather a traitor. Southerners consider Lincoln in a similar fashion. He is not our hero. It took two years for him to issue the Emancipation Proclamation (1863) despite the fact that the war is popularly depicted as one to abolish slavery. I would venture that few schools in the South are named in honor of Lincoln. On the other hand, there are quite a few named in honor of Confederate heroes. Neither group lives in a country that their ancestors chose as their patria. Despite their efforts to maintain cultural and linguistic differences, they are stigmatized as reigning backwards, harking to a perceived period of autonomous glory that the rest of the country disparages. The rapidly increasing industrialization of the South and the influx of Northern retirees to the Sunshine Belt attest to the fact that the New South will never return to the stereotypical grandeur of the Old South. Cuban-Americans who did enjoy a privileged, plantation society lifestyle will never return to that lifestyle either. López-Cruz propses that, "Está claro que Fernández no ofrece posibilidades a la supervivencia de la cultura cubana en el sur de la Florida. El autor propone una paulatina asimilación del individuo quedándose rezagados aquéllos que no logren una integración" (20). The same may be said of Southern culture as it assimilates into the mainstream to avoid feelings of cultural marginalization.

In conclusion, I think we have to look back to the idea of the so-called waves of Cubans that have emigrated to the United States. Wave is an appropriate word since it is so fully charged with meaning. As it is currently used, it is more like an *oleada*. But waves crash on the beach and the undertow pulls them back into the ocean. These immigrants cannot return to the ocean though. A more appropriate definition would be <u>holas</u> since they are really saying hello to a new life. Related to this is their patriotic fervor that is most obvious in waving the flag, which would translate as *ondear* or *flamear*. Is it a coincidence that Amber Marie's mother is named Wavene, which could be a Southern deformation of waving, as apocope occurs when the final *g* is dropped?

This is yet one more similarity between Southerners and Cubans: the dropping of initial and final consonants. Wavene also appears in *Holy Radishes!*, where she seeks to recreate the culture of the ante-bellum South. To me, the differences between Southerners and Cuban-Americans are not so disparate since both groups chop their words, come from a plantation heritage, reinvent their identities, and whose villains, Lincoln and Castro, are both defined by their beards. Both groups refuse to relinquish the flags of a bygone era. Both will continue to wave them even though their children may not know their significance because they have become traditions devoid of immediate urgency to them. This is the last legacy of exile: nostalgia gives way to oblivion as the sea of memories turns into the river of Lethe.

William O. Deaver, Jr.
ARMSTRONG ATLANTIC STATE UNIVERSITY

Works Cited

Alvarez-Borland, Isabel. *Cuban-American Literature of Exile: From Person to Persona.* Charlottesville: UP of Virginia, 1998.

Carpentier, Alejo. *El reino de este mundo.* México: Compañía General de Ediciones, 1971.

Deaver, William O. Jr. "*Raining Backwards*: Colonization and the Death of a Culture." *The Americas Review* 1 (Spring 1993): 112-118.

Faulkner, William. *The Sound and the Fury.* New York: Vintage Books, 1954.

Fernández, Roberto G. "Is in the Stars (For Lisa Photos)." *Callaloo* 1 (2001): 64-66.

———. *Holy Radishes!* Houston: Arte Público Press, 1995.

———. *Raining Backwards.* Houston: Arte Público Press, 1988.

———. *La montaña rusa.* Houston: Arte Público Press, 1985.

———. *La vida es un special.* Miami: Ediciones Universal, 1981.

Ibieta, Gabriella. "Transcending the Culture of Exile: *Raining Backwards.*" *Literature and Exile.* David Bevan, ed. Amsterdam: Rodopi, 1990. 67-75.

Irizarry, Guillermo B. "Roberto G. Fernández." *Latino and Latina Writers.* Volume II. Alan West-Durán, ed. New York: Charles Scribner's Sons, 2004. 591-611.

López-Cruz, Humberto. "Dos novelas cubanoamericanas: Dos inserciones del imaginario Cuba dentro de la realidad estadounidense." *Torre de papel* 2-3 (Summer-Fall 2003): 15-23.

Pérez, Henry. "Generational Conflicts in *Raining Backwards* by Roberto G. Fernández." *Publications of the Arkansas Philological Association* 26 (Fall 2000): 33-44.

Pérez-Firmat, Gustavo. *Cincuenta lecciones del exilio y del desexilio*. Miami: Ediciones Universal, 2000.

_____. *Life on the Hyphen: The Cuban-American Way*. Austin: UTP, 1994.

Petty, Tom. *Southern Accents*. MCA, 1985.

Suárez, Virgil and Delia Poey, eds. Introduction. *Little Havana Blues: A Cuban-American Literature Anthology*. Houston: Arte Público Press, 1996.

Vásquez, Mary S. "Family, Generation, and Gender in Two Novels of Cuban Exile: Into the Mainstream?" *The Bilingual Review/La Revista Bilingüe* 16 (1991): 23-34.

Cuban; American Literature
Suspicion of a Rupture in the Assimilation Pattern?

> It is a dangerous thing to forget the climate of your
> birthplace to choke out the voices of dead relatives when
> in dreams they call you by your secret name.
>
> Judith Ortiz Cofer

The idea of projecting a discourse of assimilation has been pursued by a vast majority of Hispanic writers in the United States. The American Dream has been everyone's goal in the fight to survive and adapt to a new way of life; for some, this life may very well begin upon setting foot on American soil. Most Hispanic writers have disguised their own experiences under their characters' struggle to adapt to their recently-acquired customs; others, have offered the readers believable individuals who have carefully observed society from various angles while, in the process, becoming a part of what up to this point has seemed to be the other side of the equation. Cuban-American literature has not deviated from the established course, but an unexpected projection in the works of two prominent Cuban-American fiction writers suggests that perhaps the authors intend to digress from the previous pattern and present a curious and uncommon outcome.

It is clear that Cuban-American literature may be grouped in various categories depending on several factors that must be considered at the time of any classification; among them is the length of time since departing from the island of birth, the language used by a particular writer, and his or her level of assimilation to American culture. The national imaginary has been recreated and modified according to the needs of each wave of Cubans that arrives to American shores. This essay explores the works of two individuals who left Cuba at a young age and during the early stages of the Cuban Revolution; their literature reflects their depiction of the Nation's imaginary; a vehicle that exposes a transplanted culture. Roberto G. Fernández (1951) and Virgil Suárez (1961) have put forward a vision of the Cuban-American dilemma on American soil from very different points of view; however, regardless of their dissimilar approaches, their conclusions have seemed directed towards a gradual integration. Carolina Hospital has developed the classification of what she calls "the children of the Cuban exile" in a time frame that allows writers such as Fernández and Suárez to fall within a transcendental period of Cuba's history.[1] She recognizes that although these children were born in Cuba, they have spent most of their lives outside the Island (103-04). All of them, Cubans as they are, have lived since childhood or adolescence in several geographical areas of the United States. This exposure to both cultures facilitates their characters' knowledge of Miami's, and in general South Florida's, heterogeneous population and the manner in which they interface with both worlds. Suárez himself has stated in the introduction to his *Little Havana Blues* that: "Cuban-American literature is currently struggling to define itself within the American literary context, drawing from rhythms, flavors and landscapes born of a unique experience that has its roots in migration and exile" (9). Notwithstanding the cultural dissimilarities, it is in Fernández's *En la Ocho y la Doce*, and Suárez's *Going Under* that the reader accepts that these writers grant the Cuban presence in the United States the possibility for survival since what is perceived is a rupture from the generally expected assimilation pattern.

Gustavo Pérez Firmat revealed in his *Life on the Hyphen* (1994) the constant struggle experienced by the average Cuban-American in order to achieve a satisfactory balance between the individual's cultural duality. Nonetheless, the hyphen acted as a separator between identities; one did not deny the other, but the nationalities did not share a common ground. On this issue, Ricardo Castells concludes that "Pérez Firmat thus paints a problematical picture of Cuban émigré life, yet this viewpoint is important because it highlights the com-

---

[1] Carolina Hospital states in her introduction to *A Century of Cuban Writers in Florida* (1-26) that writers such as Suárez and Fernández have been raised primarily in exile or in Cuba during the revolution. One important aspect that Hospital recalls is that "because of the variety of experiences, this is probably the most linguistically heterogeneous group" (25). Hospital's and Jorge Cantera's–coeditor of the text–contribution has been significant in an effort that literature by Cuban writers in Florida does not remain unnoticed.

plex nature of a community that has yet to resolve the fundamental question of its permanent relationship with its native land and–in many cases–with its adopted country" (34). But it is not until Firmat's *Cincuenta lecciones de exilio y desexilio* (2000), which may be read a conscientious summary of some of his previous writings, that the author condenses his experiences in the continuous clash of two cultures. Pérez Firmat attempts to explain the exile's search for self affirmation in society, but most importantly, he offers a logical perspective on that fictitious, yet extremely real space–for many considered a state of cultural limbo–found in the forced intersection of Cuban and American cultures. Each of the fifty lessons provides an avenue, inevitably forking when a viable solution appears on the horizon, leaving doubt after the completion of the fiftieth chapter, as to whether the author's expedition through fifty lessons, that now have become islands in an attempt to locate Cuba, was worthwhile. But it is through this questioning that the Cuban-American presence finds an opportunity to survive a bit longer and, at the same time, this suspicion provides a credible angle for approaching Fernández's and Suárez's novels with the critical focus based on Pérez Firmat's assertion of the current Cuban-American reality.

In Fernández' most noteworthy novel, *Raining Backwards*, we witness the ordeal of a homogeneous group who tries to adapt their culture to the American way of life. Fernández creates a collective conscience of the Cuban community in Miami Dade County and utilizes the carnivalization of the literary discourse to attack the most venerated icons, customs and traditions enjoyed and preserved by Cubans in South Florida.[2] Taking into consideration that "[t]he national subject splits in the ethnographic perspective of culture's contemporaneity and provides both a theoretical position and a narrative authority for mar-

---

[2] The best example is the distortion that Varadero Beach suffers when the memories are passed to younger generations–in exile–who never had the opportunity to experience the beauty of Varadero by themselves. In *Raining Backwards*, Fernández ridicules a culture that assumes such unreal visions of a beach basing its foundation on a hyperbole in order to maintain its traditions from one generation to another. Refer to the chapter "Retrieving Varadero" (11-19) for a better understanding of this concept. Moreover, note how the aforementioned concept develops into the creation of a virtual reality; Fernández, through his recurring character, Mirta, does not omit a detail during the orchestration of the parody. See López Cruz's article on this issue. On a curious note, Fernández published concurrently a Spanish version of this chapter as "El bazar de los recuerdos," *Mariel* 2.5 (1988): 8-9.

ginal voices or minority discourse" (Bhabha 301) then one can conclude that the characters in Fernández's novel make an unfruitful attempt to create a center from the margin, thus splitting their cultural perspective; the outcome will not be promising. The *Raining Backwards*' reader infers an inexorable acculturation of the young Cuban community into the American mainstream. In the clash of two worlds, the Cuban essence in the United States will die out with the older generations; it will be absorbed by the local and powerful dominating culture. During an interview with Wolfgang Binder, Fernández expressed that as time passes and the more Cubans in South Florida try to remember, the further away they get from reality; "what you have at the end is a complete mythical ending with the reinvention of the past" (119). This mythification of an uncertain past is what Fernández destroys in *Raining Backwards*; by ridiculing parameters established by the previous generation he confirms the false terrain on which the myth has been constructed. Isabel Álvarez Borland corroborates this point indicating that the old and young characters' hope rests not only how on they live, but on what they can imagine (102). The novel projects a view of demythification and, at the same time, vaticinates a gradual assimilation of Little Havana's residents into the American *melting pot*.

Raining Backwards has many examples on which the reader may base the previous conclusions; Fernández develops his plot, from the social and political spheres, in a familiar environment that allows him the possibility to subvert and parody scenes that simply happen around him. For example, the reader may focus on one of the last and more relevant stories, which appears in this novel, "Tatiana" (213). Here is resumed a characteristic seen, up to this point, in Fernández's works: the disappearance of the Cuban culture in the United States. The conversation between a grandfather and his granddaughter on a sea shore exemplifies how the author places both generations. Grandpa, blind and supposedly a war hero, wants the girl to point him in the direction of Cuba in order to take in the breeze coming from the island. In spite of his patriotism, the granddaughter associates her ancestors' homeland with a restaurant where the stench of onion, garlic, and grease fills the air. The concept of Nation transforms itself into an olfactory sensation for the new generations; Cuba's imaginary has suffered an emotional rupture without a possibility of a return to what it was only two generations ago. William Luis indicates that "[t]he recent Cuban exiles refused to give up their identity and assimilate into US society; they believed the return to the island was imminent" (149). Moreover, William O. Deaver calls the members of this group *ahogados* (117) for their inability to adapt to the new society. Fernández does not seem to allow the survival of individuals of Grandpa's generation; the blind Grandfather cannot see his own reality and symbolically drowns, *ahogado* on land, for not accepting the path of assimilation.

Other characters suffer a similar fate, but only a couple will be examined so as not to deviate from the purpose of this essay. Grandma, in her desire to return to Cuba on a self-constructed canoe, mistakes the intended course to the south and the reader assumes that the old lady perishes frozen somewhere in the North Atlantic. Mirta, after reproducing Varadero Beach in her own bathtub, ends up homeless living at the expense of others' alms. After these examples of the individuals' self destruction in Fernández's narrative, the publication of *En la Ocho y la Doce*–the intersection of these two streets symbolizes an integral space linked to the Cuban presence in Miami–constitutes a genuine surprise. A superficial reading of this series of short stories may seem, at first, a return to the author's early works;[3] in fact, some of the vignettes inserted in *En la Ocho y la Doce* have been previously published.[4] However, a significant characteristic of this new publication is that it has been written entirely in Spanish; Fernández had not offered any work in this language since the days of *La vida es un special* (1987). The return to the author's native tongue may suggest another change in his career as a writer. But more important is the chapter entitled "La gira" ("The Tour") (86-99) which constitutes irrefutable proof of Fernández's rupture with his usual conceptual approach. The reader infers that the author is either modifying his previous assimilation patterns or

---

[3] I refer to *Cuentos sin rumbo* (1975), *La montaña rusa* (1985), *La vida es un special* (1987), *Raining Backwards* (1988), and *Holy Radishes!* (1995).

[4] Most of these vignettes were published as part of *La vida es un special* (1987) or *Raining Backwards* (1988). It should also be noted that "Wrong Channel," now part of *En la Ocho y la Doce*, 12-13), first appeared in Jerome Stern's *Micro Fiction* (New York and London: W.W. Norton & Company, 1996) 30-31.

that Fernández, having run out of narrative possibilities, has decided to continue plowing a well-known field of his literary trajectory.

In spite of this speculation, "La gira" appears to be the most complete short story having, as usual, the satiric tone always recognizable in the author's works. It narrates the excursion that two of Fernández's recurring characters take to an Anglo reservation located on what used to be South Miami; they are Manolo and Barbarita who, although previously dead or handicapped, now reappear alongside other members of the Cuban community in this organized outing. The collective victim is the American community–expelled by the Cubans and forced to remain within the limits of their invented city–which lacks the basic necessities as a result of a supposed blockade imposed by the Cubans in Miami. The story recalls that the residents suffer from a continuous thirst for fear of being poisoned–the aqueduct is located on the Cuban side of the wall. This is why the Americans happily accept the donations offered by tourists; interestingly enough this hyperbolic altruism comes for the most part from Cubans while visiting the reservation. "La gira" reverses the roles, destroying the assumed archetype, and allows the Cuban presence in the United States to stay a while longer. The implied assimilation in *Raining Backwards* seems to have initiated a regressive process. The reduced space to which the American sector is confined harbors a small conglomerate that fights for survival in order to avoid becoming part of the Cuban majority; the rules have been inverted and now the community that seemed destined to fade away is the one that exercises control.

On the other hand, Suárez's *Going Under* seems at first a repetition of an established pattern: Xavier Cuevas, has succeeded in the land of opportunity, a place where he was brought by his parents at a young age and which, subsequently, has become his country. He is a young, successful and upwardly mobile businessman who projects various binary oppositions: he lives a very fast life yet seems to go nowhere; he drives a powerful Volvo, but has difficulties navigating the traffic; the day does not seem to have enough hours for his work which is to make money. He is the son of Cuban emigrants and speaks perfect English with no trace of his Latin roots. Xavier becomes irritated when his business partner, who also grew up in the States but cannot lose his thick Spanish accent, calls him an *arrepentido*, embarrassed to be Cuban (18). In fact, Xavier embodies the image that he is American, as is his wife Sarah, a mirage that draws him closer to his adoptive land and away from his parents' culture. Xavier has everything, yet feels empty.

Suárez portrays his hero through a series of paradoxes in which the reader questions the veracity of his character. Suárez's and Xavier's voices are contradictory, but one soon realizes Suárez's message: Xavier, unknowingly and unwittingly, has been trapped within the intersection of two opposite worlds. He "couldn't help but feel like an inadequate go-between: an ill-equipped translator between two cultures" (17). Xavier lives in Miami, deals with *Latinos*; yet he insists that his name be spelled and pronounced with an 'X' as opposed to the Spanish version, *Javier*.[5] If Xavier's struggle, observed during the first half of *Going Under*, is compared to *Raining Backwards*' characters one can notice that there is an established behavior in their development: the cyclical pattern of assimilation. There are very few indications that the ending will differ from *Raining Backwards*', however, Suárez offers a surprisingly contradictory twist that merits further consideration.

In the narrative, Xavier's anxiety grows as the text progresses. From the feeling of emptiness he develops a sense of solitude; he is fenced in within the very thin space where two worlds converge. Sociologically, he may belong to both, yet he cannot fully identify with either. This makes him a stranger in a

---

[5] It is important to keep in mind that the novel indicates that since Xavier was an infant when he and his family left Cuba, English became the language of his choice, and his parents occasionally spoke it at home (138). Jules Chametzky notes the language situation as the first of his six basic proposals of America's ethnic and immigrant mix when explains that "national and ethnic identification frequently arose in the U.S. precisely as a response to American conditions. It was a social and psychological need for uprooted and fragmented people to be sustained by a sense of a common experience, shared especially with those who spoke a common language" (45). And language was Xavier's first tangible step in his conquest of the new land. During his childhood no one made fun of him at school because he did not look like an outsider; he gradually became more American, less Cuban (138). As Suárez further indicates "this was his place. His country. He'd been here ninety-nine percent of his life; but the one percent couldn't be ignored [...]. That one percent made all the difference" (138). This one percent justifies the textual rupture that requires the reader to accompany the author in a radical twist. Behind this one percent, Suárez hides another possibility for the emigrant and the survival of his own identity. Contrary to the majority of Latino stories, Suárez suggests that the rupture emerges from the almost-completed acculturation process to the life in the States. It should be noted that on his *Cincuenta lecciones...*, Pérez Firmat concurs that a language is a lens through which we look and see ourselves (Lesson XVII 44), and most importantly, affirms that a language defines a place (Lesson V 18).

familiar land; he knows how to function, but fails to become part of his own created world. The pillars long embedded in American soil begin to shake, threatening the structure of his existence. Xavier has a peculiar way of solving his problems. The more he detaches himself from his daily life–absorbed by the *mare magnum* of his thoughts–the more his path deviates from the set course. The "X" with which he spells his name represents the search for the 'x', essential in solving the equation of his life; his absence from reality will be his key to identifying his own authenticity. He needs his past in order to face his future; the regression in the Xavier's behavior indicates that the acculturation process has not fully succeeded. Studies dealing with this issue have concluded that:

> social factors involved in acculturation and subsequent target language acquisition consist of social dominance patterns (dominance versus no dominance), integration strategies (assimilation versus adaptation versus preservation), enclosure, cohesiveness, size, congruence, attitude, and the intended length of residence in the target setting. (Alptekin 818)

In Xavier's case all factors point to his complete acculturation: full assimilation into the land of opportunity, full control of the language of the majority, and an indefinite–it is inconceivable to think otherwise–stay in his adopted country. To the reader, Suárez presents Xavier fully acculturalized and assimilated into his adoptive land; however, this is only a façade of the author's discursive method.

Xavier–just as Suárez himself–is a child of exile, a child who failed to completely bury his past. In order for Xavier to fully understand himself, he needs to search for his roots, his past, his origin. This is a reversal of the typical steps in the acculturation process; the discursive novelty begins rejecting the complete assimilation into the dominant culture. Through Xavier's refusal to become part of the American mainstream Suárez suggests that Cuban way of life in the States may continue for a longer amount of time. Contrary to the literature where the characters suffer a rupture in their lives upon arriving on American soil, in Xavier's life it occurs when the reader wrongly assumes that he is fully acculturalized. It may sound absurd, but it is precisely on the absurd that Suárez bases the text's rupture. Xavier needs to go back in time, back to his roots, back to his parents' culture, a culture he feels he must make his own. He must break with his life, his work, his wife, and most importantly, with himself. Only by taking down the barriers of a fictitious life can Xavier initiate a reverse metamorphosis aimed at revealing the true *Javier*, a cultural notion buried since childhood.

Xavier exemplifies the concept of rupture–as do the main characters of "La gira;" a textual rupture that must occur for them to accept the link that ties them to their past. Suárez and Fernández, as Cuban-Americans, realize they need to come to terms with their past in order to understand the future; to look for a reconciliation with their pasts means, in the case of Fernández, to resurrect his dead characters in an attempt to bring back the essence of a culture condemned by his previous writings to oblivion; in the case of Suárez, to suggest the birth of a grown-up man who has to cut the umbilical cord from his current existence to embrace his true self–or at least to make an effort to reach what he now thinks it is his true identity. Octavio Paz recounts the constant struggle of mankind throughout his life experiences in a way through which the reader can relate to the these fictional tribulations:

> When we are born we break the ties that joined us to the blind life we lived in the maternal womb, where there is no gap between desire and satisfaction. We sense the change as separation and loss, as abandonment, as a fall into a strange or hostile atmosphere. Later this primitive sense of loss becomes a feeling of solitude, and still later it becomes awareness: we are condemned to live alone, but also to transcend our solitude, to re-establish the bonds that united us with life in a paradisiacal past. (195)

Xavier's reverse metamorphosis must dissolve the element of his assimilation so that he might dissimilate from his current state. Throughout his existence, he has been constructing the emptiness of his life. The flashes that brighten his eyes while watching a sunset in his own backyard take him back in time and awaken long-forgotten memories that advise and encourage Xavier to find a new identity (137). The definite rupture coincides with the end of the novel; Xavier senses that the answers to his problems lie to the south, and in that direction he focuses his life:

> [w]ithout a map or a compass, Xavier headed south to the most southernmost point of the United States, born out of sand and water and palm trees and mangroves. The mangroves merged in a flickering blur of green as he sped. He drove with a great sense of urgency. [...] The island of his birth lay 90 miles away. Xavier remembered some of his clients saying that they drove down here because on clear, windless nights, one could see the lights from Havana. [...] Xavier stood and gazed at the open sea. [...] clothes and all, dove off and plunged into the water. He went under, opened his eyes to the sting of the salt, held his breath, and swam. (153-55)

This is the end of an era and leads to the possibility of a new beginning. In his attempt to find himself, Xavier neither departs nor perishes; the futility of his endeavor substantiates his life in the intersection between two cultures. It is the *life-on-the-hyphen* suggested by Pérez Firmat.[6] The questions the reader must face, of course, are hypothetical: What will the Cubans in Fernández's tour do when continuing to interact with Americans inside or outside their invisible-but-always-present boundaries? And, what will Xavier feel when he surfaces from the waters of the Strait? In addition, and addressing a dilemma faced by a non-fictional character, what will happen when Pérez Firmat comes out of his self-imposed exile in his own study, and returns to the family-shared spaces within his house, after completing his fiftieth lesson?

The Cubans in "La gira" will go back to their environment infatuated by a fake accomplishment that will crumble as soon as it is challenged by any interaction with a bilingual, bicultural environment. As part of the same interview with Binder, Fernández admitted that during his first couple of years in the States, his mother never unpacked, keeping the suitcases ready for an upcoming return to Cuba (107). For Manolo and Barbarita, who will keep reappearing in Fernández's narrative as long as the Cuban reality in South Florida requires it, a return to the island continues not to be a feasible option, thus explaining the need to be a part of the adopted society; in spite of this contention, com-

---

[6] This refers to Pérez Firmat's notion of a life between two cultures without fully belonging to one in particular. See *Life on the Hyphen: The Cuban-American Way* for examples and the evolution of Firmat's concept within the Cuban-American community in the United States.

plete assimilation appears to be equally unlikely. The hyphen's endeavor reflects inclusion rather than exclusion; there is no separation, but rather unification. The same may be observed in *Going Under*; by Xavier's metaphorically *going under* in the waters of the Florida Straits he proves that the new man that will emerge several seconds later will not belong to a specific shore of the Straits, but will fit in both; he dove in thinking in a tongue, as Pérez Firmat indicates, learned in childhood and then forgotten or abandoned (*Tongue Ties* 14), and surfaces, as does Firmat, longing for English as a drowning man gasps for oxygen (*Cincuenta...* 13). Suárez's character is just an entity in the middle joined in communion with the waters that bathe both shores, both cultures, without claiming supremacy over any one in particular; in order to exist, Xavier or *Javier*, must coexist with the other side of his identity, and as long as he interacts in a bilingual/bicultural society there will always be another perspective for his social placement.

As far as Pérez Firmat is concerned, the reader may speculate that he does not return defeated from his labyrinthine trip across fifty lessons of his life, yet he is satisfied even though he has not found an island that looks like his. The objects that surrounded his study at the beginning of *Cincuenta lecciones*–which had taken Spanish names in an effort to create an environment emulating a virtual reality–slowly regain their names in English (123); after a tempestuous flood, the waters recede to their river bed, knowing where they belong. The reader confirms that Pérez Firmat returns to his American everyday life where Cuba is a daily remembrance reflected in the image of his own mirror; furthermore, Firmat's conclusions in the fiftieth lesson implicitly underline his previous statement: "for good or for bad, I exist in two languages" (*El año que viene...* ii); this asseveration could not be more appropriate.

As a final consideration, it is imperative to consider if, grammatically, those who experience the tribulation of a symbolic swim across the Florida Straits should allow the possibility of an additional punctuation mark; in other words, in a multicultural and multiethnic society a *multigrammatical* option should not sound preposterous: the hyphen needs an adjacent assistant denoting the fusion of two identities.[7] One concludes that the usage of a semicolon may indicate two complex terms, two juxtaposed ideas, two independent clauses united in the same sentence, but with their own characteristics fighting to reconcile themselves. Cuban; American. In this equation solving for the mythical "x," one term cannot cancel the other; they need each variable in order to survive within a shared space. It seems that Fernández and Suárez have insinuated this possible reconciliation: the acceptance of a rupture, a deviation that has permeated the usual blueprints for assimilation. The American *melting pot* will need to wait longer for the Cuban ingredient from Miami as one of its elements; instead, it will have the addition of another tile as part of the American social mosaic. The suitcases for the return remain open, providing space for the suggested rupture in the assimilation pattern; these emblematic suitcases appear either half full or half empty. Time, once again, will have the last word.

Humberto López Cruz
UNIVERSITY OF CENTRAL FLORIDA

WORKS CITED

Alptekin, Cem. "Target Language Acquisition through Acculturation: EFL Learners in the English-speaking Environment." *The Canadian Modern Language Review* 39.4 (1983): 818-26.

Álvarez Borland, Isabel. *Cuban-American Literature of Exile: From Person to Persona*. Charlottesville and London: UP of Virginia, 1998.

Bhabha, Homi K. "DissemiNation: Time, Narrative and the Margins of the Modern Nation." *Nation and Narration*. Ed. Homi K. Bhabha. London and New York: Routledge, 1990. 291-322.

Binder, Wolfgang. "Roberto G. Fernández: An Interview". *Americas Review* 22 (1994): 106-22.

Castells, Ricardo. "*Next Year in Cuba*: Gustavo Pérez Firmat and the Rethinking of the Cuban-American Experience". *SECOLAS Annals* 30 (1999): 28-35.

---

[7] Pérez Firmat grants the possibility of another punctuation mark in his XXVI lesson (63): the slash (/); however, the connotation is the opposite; not union, but disunion. It is possible to weigh this concept with an analysis by José Piedra on Firmat's works where the critic expresses "[t]his self-consciously open closure emerges, as best, as a bilingual tantrum" (77). It is evident that what prevails is an ambiguous relation between two cultures when one intends to overshadows the other's space.

Chametzky, Jules. "Some Notes of Immigration, Ethnicity, Acculturation." *Melus* 11.1 (1984): 45-51.

Deaver, William O. *Raining Backwards*: Colonization and the Death of a Culture". *Americas Review* 21.1 (1993): 112-18.

Fernández, Roberto. *En la Ocho y la Doce*. Boston and New York: Houghton-Mifflin, 2001.

———. *Raining Backwards*. Houston: Arte Público, 1988.

Hospital, Carolina. "Los hijos del exilio cubano y su literatura." *Explicación de textos literarios* 15.2 (1986-1987): 103-14.

Hospital, Carolina and Jorge Cantera, eds. *A Century of Cuban Writers in Florida*. Sarasota: Pineapple Press, 1996.

López Cruz, Humberto. "A Technological Novelty in *Raining Backwards*: The Creation of a Virtual Reality." *Americas Review* 24.3-4 (1996): 191-200.

Luis, William. *Dance between Two Cultures*. Nashville and London: Vanderbilt UP, 1997.

Paz, Octavio. *The Labyrinth of Solitude*. Trans. Lysander Kemp. New York: Grove Press, 1961.

Pérez Firmat, Gustavo. *El año que viene estamos en Cuba*. Houston: Arte Público, 1997.

———. *Cincuenta lecciones de exilio y desexilio*. Miami: Ediciones Universal, 2000.

———. *Life on the Hyphen. The Cuban-American Way*. Austin: U of Texas P, 1994.

———. *Tongue Ties*. New York: Palgrave MacMillan, 2003.

Piedra, José. "His and Her Panics." *Dispositio* 16.41 (1991): 71-93.

Poey, Delia and Virgil Suárez, eds. *Little Havana Blues: A Cuban-American Literature Anthology*. Houston: Arte Público, 1996.

Suárez, Virgil. *Going Under*. Houston: Arte Público, 1996.

Growing Old Bilingual

The title and topic of my essay were suggested by Ana Celia Zentella's *Growing Up Bilingual* (1997), a classic study of the language habits of Puerto Rican children from New York City. Some months ago I was looking at Zentella's book in connection with my course on Latino literature, when I realized that the course itself could be entitled "Growing Up Bilingual," since most of the books on my syllabus featured children or adolescents: *Hunger of Memory* (1981), *The House on Mango Street* (1983), *How the Garcia Girls Lost Their Accents* (1991), *When I Was Puerto Rican* (1993), *Dreaming in Cuban* (1992), *Drown* (1996), *American Chica* (2001). Over the last twenty or thirty years, the dominant narrative type in the imaginative writing of U.S. Hispanics has been the coming-of-age story, novels and stories about young people coping with their bifurcated cultural inheritance. Even when a novel has older protagonists, as does Oscar Hijuelos's *The Mambo Kings Play Songs of Love* (1989), the story is filtered through the eyes of an adolescent–in this instance the mambo king's nephew, Eugenio, who (as his name suggests), is the source, the genitor, of the account. Years ago I published a memoir entitled *Next Year in Cuba* (1995). The book's subtitle, added by my publisher, was: "A *Cubano's* Coming of Age in America." One of Julia Alvarez's recent books is entitled: *Once Upon a Quinceañera: Coming of Age in the U.S.A.* (2007).

Perhaps it is inevitable that an emergent literature, a literature that is coming of age, should gravitate toward coming-of-age stories, that it should find its voice through characters who themselves are maturing, advancing not only toward adulthood but, in most instances, toward assimilation. In this respect, Latino literature as a whole draws a broad allegory of its own becoming. Although Hispanic Americans have been living in this country for centuries, it was not until 1980 that the U.S. census began to use the term "Hispanic," and it was roughly around the same time that books by Latinos started to appear in the curricula of English departments. Since for the most part their authors were second-generation Hispanics who were born or grew up in this country, their voice is that of a biculturally sensitive but English-dominant adolescent who, even as she speaks for her country or culture of origin, drifts ineluctably toward integration into the mainstream. (Indeed, the telling of the story is already an indication that the assimilation has succeeded.) That is why the name of Cristina García's protagonist in *Dreaming in Cuban* is exemplary: the doubly architectonic "Pilar Puente" conveys that the character is not only the pillar that sustains the narrative but the bridge between old world and new. When Pilar concludes, after visiting Cuba, that where she really belongs is the United States, she is speaking for her author's generation.

The attention to the experience of young Latinos has tended to make us overlook that once Latinos finish growing up, they start growing old. There is another type of coming of age that is the real coming of age: the coming of old age. After all, Marie Arana's American *chica* is by now an American *vieja*. The Garcia girls, who lost their accents back in the 1960s, are now losing their teeth. And Richard Rodriguez's famous "hunger of memory" has begun to manifest itself in senior moments. Even if the Latino literary canon makes it seem that Hispanics never grow up, we do grow up; then, if we're lucky, we grow old. Fifteen years ago I wrote a book called *Life on the Hyphen* (1994) where I discussed the balancing act that characterizes the lives of many Hispanic Americans, the linguistic and ethnic hyphen that marks our place in America. As we get older, what happens to our bodies happens to our hyphen: it becomes less firm, loses its elasticity, begins to sag. It turns into a wrinkle or a scar.

And so my subject today is later-in-life on the hyphen, how the passing of time inflects the bicultural writer's work. More concretely, I'm interested in what time does to our relation with the languages we speak or write. As we get older, do our tongues age along with us? Or do we make up for other losses and diminishments by growing ever more intimate with them? How different is the slick tongue of a *quinceañera* from the slack tongue of a *cincuentón*? In a poem entitled "Dulzura," Sandra Cisneros asks her lover: "Make love to me in Spanish. / Not with that other tongue."[1] The switch in prepositions, from *"in*

---

[1] "Dulzura," in *Loose Woman* (New York: Vintage, 1995) 27.

Spanish" to "*with* that other tongue," signals how quickly tongues allow us to glide from wordplay to foreplay. As we get older, does that gliding become smoother or more difficult?

As all of you realize, a language is not only an instrument of communication. In Spanish, when one knows a language well, one is said to "dominate" it. But my mother tongue has it backwards, for however large our vocabularies, however supple our tongues, we don't dominate languages; languages dominate us. It is the language that determines the domain, the dominion, and we as speakers cannot but submit to its territorial imperatives. A language tells us what we can and cannot say, think and feel in ways of which we are not even aware. As Andrée Tabouret Keller puts it, "language acts are acts of identity."[2] We are what we speak. In *The American Scene,* Henry James remarks that a person's "supreme relation" is to his homeland, but James's own life shows that his attachment to the English language was stronger than his allegiance to the United States.[3] It may be that a person's strongest, most enduring attachment is to his language, or more precisely, to his tongue, for a tongue is language incarnate, language as a body part, an organ as well as a faculty. Although no language can match the looseness of a tongue, tongues tie in ways that languages never do. And so the languages that we possess possess us in return.

It is also well to keep in mind that a bilingual's relation to his languages is not symmetrical. In the poem I quoted a few moments ago, Cisneros asks for a tenderness that she can feel only in Spanish, a sweetness that only exists as *dulzura*. When she asks to be loved in Spanish, she's looking for another self, perhaps a former or a secret self, someone she used to be or someone she never was. That's why I'm sceptical of what is sometimes called "balanced bilingualism." Even among those who have been raised bilingually, the relation of languages is usually not balanced. The notion of a balanced bilingualism or *equilingüismo,* as it is called in Spanish, is as much of a pedagogical fiction as

---

[2] "Language and Identity," *The Handbook of Sociolinguistics,* ed. Florian Coulmas (Oxford: Blackwell, 1977) 315-26.
[3] *The American Scene* (Bloomington: Indiana University Press, 1968) 85.

that of a bilingualism without pain. Elsa Triolet, a francophone Russian writer, used to complain, "I am sick with bilingualism."[4]

Whether a burden or a blessing, bilingualism is profoundly and even mysteriously personal. And no small part of its mystery has to do with what happens to our tongues as we age. With time, a foreign language could well evolve into a conjugal tongue; the sounds that cradled us in infancy could haunt us in our old age. When we are learning a language, whether in the classroom or the bedroom, our relation with the new language is constantly evolving. Every word we learn, every sentence we speak, affects our relation with the language as a whole. As we get older, this evolution continues. We never stop learning our languages, and we never stop forgetting them. It is a little bit like an endless courtship. We are permanent suitors of language, never turned down yet never fully accepted.

Take the case of the Franco-Argentine novelist Héctor Bianciotti, who was born in Córdoba, Argentina, in 1930. Even though his Italian immigrant parents spoke the Piedmontese dialect with each other, they always spoke to their children in Spanish and insisted that their children speak only in Spanish. For this reason, Bianciotti believes that he never had a true mother tongue. Spanish was, at best, a stepmother tongue, a substitute for the real thing, which would have been the forbidden Piedmontese dialect. Until he was twenty-five Bianciotti lived in Argentina and then he left for Europe. After spending several years in Spain, in 1961 he settled permanently in France. Over the next twenty years, while residing in Paris, Bianciotti wrote and published five volumes of fiction in Spanish: *Los desiertos dorados* (1965), *Detrás del rostro que nos mira* (1969), *Ritual* (1973), *La busca del jardín* (1977), *El amor no es amado* (1983). But in 1982, after turning fifty and becoming a naturalized French citizen, something happened to his fiction: he began to write it in French; his first francophone novel, *Sans la miséricorde du Christ* (1985), appeared a couple of years later. Once he began writing fiction in French, Bianciotti stopped writing in Spanish altogether. He even stopped speaking it. By his own admission, he enclosed himself inside what he called the "delicate labyrinth" of the French

---

[4] As quoted in Elizabeth Klosky Beaujour, *Alien Tongues: Bilingual Russian Writers of the "First" Emigration* (Ithaca: Cornell University Press, 1989) 40.

tongue.[5] His career as a francophone writer culminated with his election in 1996 to the Académie Française; he was the first Latin-American-born writer to be so honored.

Bianciotti has discussed his switch from Spanish to French in several interviews as well as in his novels, which are generally autobiographical (he labels them "autofictions"). In an interview about the publication of *Sans la miséricorde du Christ,* Bianciotti explains that his Spanish has deteriorated to the point that he can no longer write in that language even if he wanted to. As he puts it, "Je ne sais pas encore si le français m'accepté; je suis certain en revanche que l'espagnol m'a peu à peu quitté" [I am not sure that French has accepted me; but on the other hand I know for certain that little by little Spanish has left me].[6] Surprisingly, Bianciotti thinks of himself as essentially tongueless–not *bilingüe* but *nilingüe,* homeless in two languages. Nonetheless, since to this day he speaks French with a thick Argentine accent, it is not strictly true that Spanish has abandoned him. Linguists tell us that among adult learners of a second language, the most persistent type of linguistic interference is phonological; it is easier to pick up a language's grammar and syntax, however complicated, than it is to reproduce its sounds. The most foreign thing about a foreign language is its voice print–the sounds and rhythms that weave its secret melody. Even if we forget all the words of our first language, our tongue remains tuned to its music. And so Bianciotti, widely regarded as a consummate stylist in French, cannot correctly pronounce the words with which he crafts his crystalline sentences.

Elsewhere Bianciotti has remarked that his two muses are nostalgia and remorse.[7] It may be that both are byproducts of the switch in languages. When Bianciotti looks back to his youth, as he does in his most of his francophone fiction, he is not only looking back to another time and another place, but to another language. In *Le pas si lente de l'amour* (1995), when he reminisces about his childhood in Córdoba, Argentina, the act of recollection entails an exercise in translation. By recalling in French a life that unfolded in Spanish, he

---

[5] "Discours de réception." January 23, 1997. http://academie-francaise.fr. Accessed December 21, 2007.
[6] "Changer de langue, changer de façon de'être," *La Quinzaine littéraire* 436 (March 1985): 10.
[7] "Trading Places: A Conversation with Hector Bianciotti," *Hopscotch* 1.4 (1999): 111.

makes all the more evident his distance from that life. Bianciotti's nostalgia arises not only from the memories of people and places but from the memory of sounds which he no longer hears even if his tongue remains in their thrall. When he states that "en revanche" (literally, in revenge) for his adoption of French Spanish has all but abandoned him, the phrase hints at the guilt that accompanies his use of the French language. Spanish avenges the switch in loyalties by making itself unavailable, as if saying to Bianciotti: leave me, lose me.

For a hyphenate writer like Bianciotti, who obsessively mines his past, the discomfort of expressing himself in a foreign language only increases with age. The fluency and record of achievement in the second language do nothing to diminish the unease, for its origins are not linguistic but lingual: they are tied to a tongue rather than to a language.[8] Although Bianciotti likes to say that he never had a mother tongue, I suspect the denial is a way of muffling his remorse at having abandoned Spanish, his mother (if not his mother's) tongue. It is true, at least, that he thinks of writing in French as an illicit or shady activity, often comparing it to a kind of contraband. In no less of an occasion than his acceptance speech at the Academie Française, he confesses that he entered the French language, "par des chemins de contrebandier," "through the paths of smugglers."[9]

Bianciotti's last book in Spanish, *El amor no es amado* (1983), includes "La barca en el Néckar," a story centering on the sixty-five year old janitor of a Parisian apartment house. After his wife dies, the old man has nothing to do except spend his time straightening out the garbage cans, sweeping the stairs, watering the plants–and remembering. Twenty years earlier he had been part of the German forces that occupied Paris during World War II. After falling in love with the French woman who became his wife, he deserted and stayed in France. Now that he is alone, the old man lies awake in his basement apartment thinking back to his early years in Tübingen, when his ambition had been to become a poet, another Hölderlin. Recalling his youth, he realizes that his

---

[8] For the distinction between "tongue" and "language," see my *Tongue Ties: Logo-Eroticism in Anglo-Hispanic Literature* (New York: Palgrave Macmillan, 2003) 14-20.
[9] "Discours de réception." January 23, 1997. http://academie-francaise.fr. Accessed December 21, 2007.

native tongue has slipped away from him, and with it the young man he used to be, for "el muchacho no había sido más que el idioma que hablara y que su idioma no era para mí, ahora, más que una nebulosa oculta" [the boy was only his language and his language was now for me nothing more than a hidden nebula].[10]

Although this story was published in Spanish, it was originally written in French. In fact, "La barca en el Néckar" was Bianciotti's first piece of French fiction. This suggests that the old man is Bianciotti's double, his metaphor for the writer who "deserts," who abandons his mother tongue for another tongue. It does not matter that in the story the acquisition of a conjugal tongue compensates for the loss of the childhood language. The old man's status as a deserter makes clear Bianciotti's feelings about the switch. As a valedictory to Spanish, Bianciotti's inaugural performance in French not only evinces nostalgia for his mother tongue–a proleptic nostalgia, a nostalgia *avant la lettre,* as it were–but also shows the emotional toll extracted by the abandonment or forgetting of a first language, which appears to the deserter as distant as a nebula. He muses to himself: "Ahora mi conducta me da vergüenza y a veces me pregunto por qué motivo me convertí en desertor" [Now my conduct makes me ashamed and I ask myself why I became a deserter].[11] It may be that Bianciotti, as he was launching his career as a francophone novelist, asked himself the same question.

Bianciotti's portrait of the bilingual artist as an old man comports with my own experience. Like his deserter, I feel nostalgia for my mother tongue and remorse that I have not done more of my writing, and perhaps my living, in Spanish. Sometimes I have even thought that every single one of my English sentences, including this one, covers up the absence of the Spanish sentence that I wasn't willing or able to write. And if I handle English more or less well, it is because I want to write such clear, clean prose that no one will miss the Spanish that it replaces, and that it can never replace. (I would not be surprised if a similar ambition lay behind Bianciotti's spotless French prose.) For most of my adult life, the language I have felt uneasy about has been Spanish, not Eng-

---

[10] *El amor no es amado* (Barcelona: Tusquets, 1983) 215.
[11] *El amor no es amado* (Barcelona: Tusquets, 1983) 212.

lish; my birth tongue, not my adopted language. Criticize my English, and your words will never touch me. Criticize my Spanish, and you're undermining my deepest convictions and theories about myself. "If you want to hurt me," writes Gloria Anzaldúa, "talk badly about my language."[12] For me, that language is Spanish.

There is an *I love Lucy* episode in which Lucy hires an English tutor to improve Ricky's pronunciation. At this point in the series Lucy is pregnant with Little Ricky, and she is afraid that their son will pick up his father's pronunciation. The English tutor, a man called Mr. Livermore, is a stuffy, bow-tied pedant with an affected pronunciation and a hysterical aversion to slang. During the first lesson, Mr. Livermore instructs his class, which of course also includes Lucy, Fred and Ethel, on the correct pronunciation of the English vowels. Unlike his classmates, who imitate Livermore's fastidious enunciation well enough, Ricky pronounces the vowels in Spanish: "ah," "eh," "ee," "oh," "oo." Mr. Livermore can't believe his ears. Stunned, he turns to Ricky: "Mr. Ricardo," he says, "wherever did you acquire that odd pronunciation?" And Ricky replies: "I'm Cuban, what's *your* excuse?" Well, I'm Cuban too, and so to the Mr. Livermores of my life, to those who may criticize my English, I can always reply, "I'm Cuban, what's your excuse?" But I cannot dispose of criticisms of my Spanish so lightly.

According to E. M. Cioran, a Rumanian who wrote mostly in French, our mother tongue is the only one in which we have a right to make mistakes. But for those of us who tie our identity to our nationality (as exiles tend to do), and our nationality to our tongue (as exiles also do), exactly the opposite is true: our mother tongue is the one language in which we *cannot* make mistakes. Since a crucial component of our self-image is the idea we have of ourselves as language users, one of the most disabling forms of self-doubt arises from the conviction that we cannot speak our native language well enough. As I have gotten older, I have become more willing to admit in public to mother-tongue separation-anxiety. I think I have gained a better understanding of its causes and occasions, and my lingual superego, my Spanish-speaking *conciencia,* treats

---

[12] Gloria Anzaldúa, *Borderlands: The New Mestiza,* 2nd ed. (San Francisco: Aunt Lute Books, 1999) 81.

me less harshly than it used to. At the same time, like Bianciotti's deserter, I have also become more aware of the void created by the absence of Spanish.

Some years ago, I decided that it wasn't too late to reach out and back to my mother tongue. So I wrote a little book in Spanish, about Spanish, a combination language proficiency test and belated love poem (*Cincuenta lecciones de exilio y desexilio,* 2000). I have never written more easily, or with more ease. Every word I used seemed newly minted–and newly minted for me. Just putting accents was a thrill, generating an ñ an occasion for celebration. Every time I got lost inside one of those expansive periods of Spanish sentences, I relished the adventure. Somehow, I always found my way out. When I write in English, I write silently, hearing the words only in my head. Composing Spanish sentences, I found myself sounding out each word, reciting each sentence as I wrote or rewrote it. The pleasure was lingual rather than merely linguistic. It was tied to a tongue rather than to a language. What I felt was something like an *acorde,* a consonance, between my tongue and my ear, as if the two organs had finally met their match. I felt so comfortable in my mother tongue, so surprisingly at home in my home, that I wondered how I could have spent all those years in someone else's dwelling. Compared to Spanish, English offered bare accommodations, little more than four walls and a roof over my head–an abode not unlike the deserter's Paris apartment. But Spanish was my homestead, somewhere I could settle for life. I swore to myself that I had written my last English sentence.

Evidently, since I'm speaking to you in English today, I did not live up to my loyalty oath. Soon after finishing my Spanish book, I began to miss English. I began to miss words like "miss." I began to miss words like "word," so different from the Spanish *palabra,* which in English is only palaver. But my point is that, whatever the compensations, nostalgia for and remorse over a lost or neglected language is one of the most enduring legacies of exile. In all the years that I've lived in the United States, there has not been a day when I have not heard a word of English, but there have been many, many days when I have not heard a word of Spanish.

Not long ago I spent an afternoon going through a little book of *cubanismos,* Cuban words and idioms, published in Miami in the 1960s. It struck me that I hadn't heard many of those expressions in decades, and that I may never hear them again. Twenty years ago, there was nobody in my family with whom I did not speak in Spanish. Today I speak in Spanish only with my mother. A few years from now, I will speak Spanish only with myself. Lose the words, lose the world. Although we tend to think of the course of human life as circular–ashes to ashes, dust to dust–for exiles and immigrants the course of our lives is not circular at all, since the sounds that cradled us at birth are not those that surround us as we grow old. And yet somehow our birth language never goes completely silent. It keeps ringing in our inner ear, asking us to pick up and listen.

Bianciotti's writing once again offers a vivid illustration. Both in interviews and in his fiction Bianciotti has frequently mentioned the changes that an object undergoes according to the language that names it. His favorite examples are the French and Spanish words for bird: *oiseau* and *pájaro*. As he writes in one of his novels, "Si je dis *oiseau*, j'éprouve que les voyelles que sépare en les caressant le *s*, créent une petite bête tiède, au plumage lisse et luisant, qui aime son nid; en revanche, si je dis *pájaro*, à cause de l'accent de intensité que soulève la premiére syllabe, l'oiseau espagnol fend l'air comme une flèche" [If I say *oiseau*, I notice that the vowels that surround the *s*, caressing it, evoke a warm, small creature, with smooth and shining plumage, a creature that loves its nest. On the other hand, if I say *pájaro*, because of the accent on the first syllable, the Spanish bird pierces the air like an arrow].[13] He adds that since he prefers closed spaces to open ones, the garden to the pampa, he is more like the French *oiseau* than like the Spanish *pájaro*.

But consider now the title of one of Bianciotti's last books: *Comme la trace de l'oiseau dans l'air* (1999), "Like the track of a bird in the air." In the context of Bianciotti's comments about the difference between *oiseau* and *pájaro*, his title is something of a solecism, for he attributes to the *oiseau* the flightiness that he identifies with the *pájaro*. In other words, Bianciotti's French *oiseau* retains the trace, the footprint, of the Spanish *pájaro*. So here we have a *rara avis* indeed: a French bird that behaves like a Spanish bird. (Mother tongues never forget: not coincidentally, Bianciotti in this passage again refers to Span-

---

[13] *Les pas si lente de l'amour* (Paris: Grasset, 1995) 330.

ish acting "en revanche.") That's why the title of the Spanish translation of the novel, *Como la huella de un pájaro en el aire,* though literally exact, fails to capture the foreignnesss, the atavism nestled in the French title. In *Les pas si lente de l'amour* Bianciotti also states the French language has "dried up" his Spanish like a vine that chokes the trunk of a tree: "tel le lierre qui s'enroule autour dún arbre il [le français] a desséché en moi l'espagnol."[14] However stressed and vine-ridden, that tree is still yielding sap, and *pájaros* have built their nests in its branches. Whether Bianciotti admits it or not, Spanish continues to influence his language use. Inside his *oiseau* there is a *pájaro* flapping its wings.

Frank Sinatra once said, memorably, "May the last voice you hear be mine." The older we get, the less bilingualism is a political, social, or even linguistic issue, and the more it becomes a private affair, intimate theater. According to the poet Derek Walcott, to change your language you must change your life. But the converse is also true: A change in your language brings about a change in your life, which is why the stakes of using one language rather than another increase as we age. Bianciotti's refusal of his mother tongue expresses the desire to grow old in the company of only one tongue, the desire to speak or write at last with a voice not haunted by other voices. I'm afraid, however, that this desire, like others, has to go unsatisfied. Once bilingual, always bilingual. We can change our lives and we can change our languages, but what we cannot do is recapture the time before (or after) our tongue was forked by another tongue. Riddled by nostalgia and remorse, the bilingual muse is a melancholy muse. It divides and does not conquer. And so the best we can hope for as we age is that, unlike the German deserter, we don't become deaf to the sounds we rejoiced in before we knew that there were other languages, other sounds. Which is another way of saying: May the last voice you hear be yours.

Gustavo Pérez Firmat
COLUMBIA UNIVERSITY

---

[14] *Les pas si lente de l'amour* (Paris: Grasset, 1995) 330.

CONTRIBUTORS

PETER CARRAVETTA is the Alfonse M. D'Amato Professor of Italian and Italian American Studies at SUNY/Stony Brook. Founding editor of *Differentia, review of italian thought* (1986-1999), he has published *Prefaces to the Diaphora. Rhetorics, Allegory and the Interpretation of Postmodernity* (1991), *Il Fantasma di Hermes* (1996), *Dei Parlanti* (2002), and co-edited *Postmoderno e letteratura* (1984) and *Poeti italiani d'America* (1993). He is also the author of six books of poetry, among which *delle voci* (1980), *Metessi* (1991) and *The Sun and Other Things* (1998). He has written widely on critical theory, poetics, migration, history of ideas and cultural studies. His most recent book is *Del postmoderno. Critica e cultura nell'America di fine millennio* (Milano, Bompiani), of which an English translation is forthcoming.

DEBORA CORDEIRO ROSA received her Ph.D. in Spanish and Hispanic American Literature from Florida State University in 2005. She is currently an Assistant Professor at University of Central Florida in Orlando. Her research focus is on Jewish writers of Latin America, exploring subjects such as change /loss of identity, assimilation, acculturation, holocaust, trauma and exile. She also teaches Portuguese and writes about topics related to Brazilian culture and language. Debora has several articles and book reviews published and is working on her first book on issues of identity in the narratives of Jewish writers from the Southern Cone.

WILLIAM O. DEAVER, JR. holds a B.A. in English and an M.A. in Spanish from the University of Virginia as well as a Ph.D. in Spanish from Florida State University. He is a professor of Spanish at Armstrong Atlantic State University in Savannah, Georgia. In addition to his teaching duties, he directs the study abroad program in Mexico and the Latin American Studies Certificate. He has published articles and book chapters not only about Spanish, Spanish-American, and Cuban-American authors, but also film directors. He was also awarded a Chancellor's Award Grant to pursue research in Cuba in 2001.

GUSTAVO PÉREZ FIRMAT was born in Havana, Cuba, and raised in Miami, Florida. Firmat has been the recipient of fellowships from the National Endowment for the Humanities, the American Council of Learned Societies, the Mellon Foundation, and the Guggenheim Memorial Foundation. In 2004 he was elected to the American Academy of Arts and Sciences. A writer and scholar, he is the author of several books and numerous essays and reviews. His books of literary and cultural criticism include: *Literature and Liminality* (1986), *The Cuban Condition* (1989), *Life on the Hyphen* (1994, *Cincuenta lecciones de exilio y desexilio*(2000), and *Tongue Ties* (2003). He has also published several collections of poetry in English and Spanish In 1995, Pérez Firmat was named Duke University Scholar/Teacher of the Year, Duke University's highest award for teaching excellence. *Hispanic Business Magazine* selected him as one of the "100 most influential Hispanics" in the United States, and in 2004 he was named one of New York's thirty "outstanding Latinos" by *El Diario La Prensa*.

PAOLO A. GIORDANO is the Neil E Euliano Endowed Professor of Italian Studies (Ph.D. Indiana University in Italian) and chair of the Department of Modern Languages and Literatures at the University of Central Florida. He is co-founder and co-director of Bordighera Press and past president of the American Association of Teachers of Italian. He has published widely on Italian Renaissance literature and Italian-American studies. His books include: *Introducing Italian Americana: Generalities on Literature and Film. A Bilingual Forum* (2005); *From the Margins: Writings in Italian Americana* (2000, rev. ed.); (1998); *Esilio, Migrazione e Sogno Americano* (2001); *Ethnicity: Poems by Joseph Tusiani.* (2000). In 2004 he received the "Outstanding Alumnus Award" from his alma mater Southern Connecticut State University; and in the same year the Italian Government recognized his work in Italian Studies with the title "Cavaliere, Stella della Solidarietà Italiana."

JEFFREY S. LIBRETT is Professor of German (Ph.D. Cornell University, 1989, in Comparative Literature), as well as Head of the Department of German and Scandinavian at the University of Oregon. Professor Librett has written *The Rhetoric of Cultural Dialogue: Jews and Germans from Moses Mendelssohn to Richard Wagner and Beyond* (Stanford University Press, 2000), and published numerous essays on German literature, philosophy, psychoanalysis, Jewish Studies, and theory from the eighteenth century to the present. He has translated numerous texts from German and French into English, including Jean-Luc Nancy's *The Sense of the World* (University of Minnesota Press, 1997) and *Of the Sublime: Presence in Question,* by Michel Deguy et al (State University of New York Press, 1993). He is currently writing a book provisionally entitled *Orientalist Metaphysics: Typology and Panic in Modern German Letters.*

HUMBERTO LÓPEZ CRUZ Professor of Spanish at the University of Central Florida. Dr. López's research interests are focused on Latin American literature and culture; most specifically, in Spanish Caribbean literature, Central American literature, with a concentration on Panamanian literature where a significant number of his publications are concentrated, and the dynamic literature written by Hispanics in the United States. He has published over six books, and forty-eight articles in peer-refereed journals with several more near publication. Some of his published work deals with the XIX Century antislavery novel as a fictionalized recognition of a social reality within Cuban colonial society, reaffirming the ideological conceptions that allowed for the emergence of this type of narrative. In addition, he has numerous published book articles and reviews, and contributes regularly to newspaper articles, both domestic and international. He has published poetry in Spanish.

ANTHONY JULIAN TAMBURRI is Dean of the John D. Calandra Italian American Institute (Queens College, CUNY) and Professor of Italian and Italian/American Studies. He holds a Ph.D. from the University of California, Berkeley in Italian. He is co-director of Bordighera Press, past president of the American Italian Historical Association and the American Association of Teachers of Italian. His books include: *Italian/American Short Films & Music Videos* (2002), *Semiotics of Re-reading: Guido Gozzano, Aldo Palazzeschi, and Italo Calvino* (2003), *Narrare altrove: diverse segnalature letterarie* (2007), and *Una semiotica dell'etnicità* (2010), and, forthcoming, *Revisiting Italian Americana: Specificities and Generalities on Literature and Film.* He is also the executive producer of *Italics, The Italian American TV Magazine,* produced by the Calandra Institute and CUNY-TV. In 2000, he received the "Outstanding Alumnus Award" from his alma mater Southern Connecticut State University and, recently, he was conferred the honor of "Cavaliere dell'Ordine al Merito della Repubblica Italiana."

INDEX

Adorno, Theodor W.: 40 n.5
Alvarez-Borland, Isabel: 68
Anderson, Benedict: 58, 59
Anderson, Benedict: 66
Antonelli, Sara: 8 n.20
Anzaldúa, Gloria: 105
Arana, Marie: 99
Aristotle: 35

Bacigalupo, Massimo: 10 n.25
Baker, Houston: 11 n.26
Baldacci, David: 9
Ballerini, Luigi: 21 n.40
Barth, Theorist Fredrik: 63
Beaujour, Elizabeth Klosky: 101 n.4
Bianciotti, Hector: 101
Binder, Wolfgang: 88
Birmajer, Macelo: 66
Birmajer, Marcelo: 61
Blaisten, Isidoro: 61
Blaisten, Isidoro: 66
Bluman, Jew Saúl: 61
Bona, Mary Jo: 7 n.17, 12 n.29
Bonanno, Joe: 19
Broda, Martine: 45
Brown, Ruoff A. LaVonne: 11 n.26
Bruce-Novoa, Juan: n.26
Brunschwig, Colette: 37-55, 38 n.2, 47 n.12, 48 n.13, 50 n.16, 52 n.17
Burke, Kenneth: 35

Calandra, John D.: 16 n.34
Cannistraro, Philip V.: 18, 25 n.46
Caputo, Philip: 9

Carnevali, Emanuel: 21 n.40
Carravetta, Peter: 21 n.39, 28 n.2
Carrera, Alessandro: 21 n.40
Casella, Paola: 7 n.15
Cassirer, Ernst: 31 n.4
Castagneto, Pierangelo: 10 n.25
Castells, Ricardo: 86
Cecchetti, Giovanni: 21 n.40
Celan, Paul: 37-55, 37 n.1, 38 n.2, 38 n.3, 40 n.5, 40 n.7, 48 n.13, 50 n.15, 50 n.16, 52 n.17
Chametzky, Jules: 91 n.5
Ciardi, John: 23
Ciccarelli, Andrea: 21 n.39
Cinotto, Simone: 7 n.15
Cioran, E.M.: 105
Cisneros, Sandra: 99
Cofer, Judith Ortiz: 85
Condini, Ned: 21 n.40
Cosco, Joseph P.: 9 n.22
Craibs, Ian: 66
Craibs, Ian: 59
Cuevas, Xavier: 90

Daniels, Roger: 3 n.5
De Nonno, Tony: 25 n.46
de Salvo, Louise: 7
De Stefano, George: 23
DeLillo, Don: 7, 9
Demosthenes: 46
Derrida, Jacques: 32, 37 n.1, 42, 43 n.10, 49
di Donato, Pietro: 7
Dilthey, Wilhelm: 31 n. 4
Dinale, Rita: 21 n. 40
DiStasi, Lawrence: 3 n. 5, 6 n. 14

Dobson, F. A.: 13
Durante, Francesco: 6

Elliott, Emory: 13 n. 30

Fante, John: 7
Fernández, Roberto G.: 67
Ferraro, Evelyn: 9 n. 20
Ferraro, Thomas: 12 n. 29
Ferrucci, Franco: 21 n. 40
Fishkin, Shelley Fisher: 13 n. 30
Flora, Joseph M.: 78
Fontanella, Luigi: 21 n.39
Ford, David B.: 11
Foucault, Michel: 33
Fox, Steven R.: 3 n.5
Frasca, Simona: 7 n.15
Frazzi, Andrea: n.45
Frazzi, Antonio: 24 n.45
Freud, Sigmund: 32
Fried, Michael: 50
Frisch, Michael H.: 13 n.30
Fuss, Diana: 59

Gadamer, Hans-Georg: 31 n.4, 32
García, Cristina: 70
Gardaphè, Fred: 12 n.29, 13 n.31
Gates, Henry Louis: 11 n.26
Gehrke, Richard: 47 n.12
Gertopan, Susana: 66
Gertopan, Susana: 64
Giemza, Bryan Albin: 78
Giovannitti, Arturo: 21 n.40
Giunta, Edvige: 7 n.17, 12 n.29
Glantz, Margo: 62
Glantz, Margo: 66
Gnisci, Armando: 9 n.20
Gorlier, Claudio: 6 n.15

Goux, Jean-Joseph: 40 n.5
Basile Green, Rose: 12 n.29, 19, 19 n.37
Greenberg, Clement: 50
Griffith D. W.: 14
Grünspan, Herschel: 46
Guglielmo, Jennifer: 9 n.22, 25n.46

Halttunen, Karen: 13 n.30
Hegel, Georg W. F.: 50
Heidegger, Martin: 32
Heidegger, Martin: 42
Hendin, Josephine Gattuso: 12 n.29
Herf, Jeffrey: 40 n.5
Hijuelos, Oscar: 70
Humboldt, Wilhelm von: 35

Ibieta, Gabriella: 77
Irizarry, Guillermo B.: 77

Jacobson, Mathew: 9 n.22
Jones, Suzanne W.: 78

Kaplan, Amy: 13 n.30
Keller, Andrée Tabouret: 100
Kelley, Mary: 12 n.30
Kiefer, Anselm: 40 n.4
Krase, Jerome: 15
Krauss, Rosalind: 52 n.17

Lacoue-Labarthe, Philippe: 37 n.1
LaGumina, Salvatore: 3 n.6, 9 n.22, 14 n.33
Lang, Berel: 38 n.3
Lanzmann, Claude: 38 n.3
Lerner, Julio: 62n

Levi, Primo: 38 n.3, 49
Lévinas, Emmanuel: 37-38, 37 n.1, 38 n.2
Lispector, Clarice: 62, 62 n. 2
Lispector, Clarice: 66
Livorni, Ernesto: 21 n.40
Humberto: 69
Luconi, Stefano: 7 n.15
Luis, William: 89
Lyotard, Jean-François: 40 n.5

Maiello, Adele: 7 n.15
Mandelstam, Osip: 45
Marazzi, Martino: 7 n.18
Marchand, Jean-Jacques: 21 n.39
Marchegiani, Irene: 21 n.40
Margolis, Joseph: 32
McClintock, Anne: 29 n.3
Montero, Mayra: 70
Moroni, Mario: 21 n.40
Moses: 46
Muñoz, Elías Miguel: 70
Muscio, Giuliana: 7 n.15

Napoleon: 33
Nietzsche, Friedrich: 32, 35

Obejas, Achy: 70
Orsi, Robert: 7 n.16

Patriarca, Gianna: 24 n.45
Paulicelli, Eugenia: 21 n.40
Paz, Octavio: 93
Pérez, Henry: 67
Perez, Renard: 64 n.5
Pérez-Firmat, Gustavo: 67
Petty, Tom: 81
Photos, Lisa: 68

Piedra, José: 96 n.7
Pietralunga, Mario: 21 n.40
Plato: 35
Poey, Delia: 69
Portelli, Alessandro: 7 n.18
Porter, Edwin: 14
Pugliese, Stanislao: 25 n.46

Radhakrishnan, Rajagopalan: 30 n.1, 30
Radway, Janice A.: 12 n.30
Rath, Ernst vom: 46
Rawet, Samuel: 62
Reynolds, Manuela: 71
Rihm, Wolfgang: 50 n.15
Rimanelli, Giose: 21 n.40
Rizzardi, Alfredo: 10 n.24
Rodriguez, Richard: 99
Romeo, Caterina: 7 n.18
Roosevelt, Franklin Delano: 2
Rorty, Richard: 32
Ruiz, Vicki: 13 n.30

Saccà, Annalisa: 21 n.40
Saldivar, Ramon: 11 n.26
Salerno, Sal: 9 n.22, 25 n.46
Saltzman, Lisa: n.5
Sanchez, George: 13 n.30
Saunders, Kay: 3 n.5
Scarpino, Cinzia: 8, 8 n.20
Schiller, Friedrich: 50
Schmitt, Carl: 43
Sciorra, Joseph: 24
Scliar, Moacyr: 62
Scott, Lisa: 11
Scottoline, Lisa: 9, 11
Shirley, Carl: 11 n.26
Shirley, Paula: 11 n.26

Singer, Bashevis: 60, 60 n. 1
Singer, Isaac Bashevis: 66
Sinha, Gunjan: 66
Soprano, Tony: 14
Stefanile, Felix: 1
Suárez, Virgil: 69
Sumida, Stephen H.: 13 n.30

Takaki, Ronald: 11 n.26
Talese, Gay: 18-20, 19 n.35
Tirabassi, Maddalena: 6 n.15
Triolet, Elsa: 101
Tusiani, Joseph: 21 n.40
Tusmith, Bonnie: 11 n.26

Valesio, Paolo: 21n.39
Vásquez Mary S.: 67
Vattimo, Gianni: 32, 32 n.6
Vecoli, Rudy: 7 n.16
Vico, Giambattista: 31, 31 n.5, 35
Vieira, Nelson: 62
Vieira, Nelson: 66
Viscusi, Robert: 1, 12 n.29, 13 n.31, 15
Vogel, Amber: 78

West, Cornel: 16

Zentella, Ana Celia: 98

SAGGISTICA

Taking its name from the Italian–which means essays, essay writing, or non fiction–*Saggisitca* is a referred book series dedicated to the study of all topics, individuals, and cultural productions that fall under what we might consider that larger umbrella of all things Italian and Italian/American.

Vito Zagarrio. *The "Un-Happy Ending": The Cinema of Frank Capra Between American Dream And American Nightmar. (Re-Visioning Frank Capra, 1928-1934).* 2010. ISBN 978-1-59954-005-4. Volume 1.

The following volumes are forthcoming:

Dennis Barone
  America / Trattabili.
Fred L. Gardaphè
  The Art of Reading Italian Americana.
Anthony Julian Tamburri
  Revisiting Italian Americana. Specificities and Generalities on Literature and Film